ISBN 978-1-934655-31-3

06-020 • COPYRIGHT © 1986 **World Evangelism Press**®
P.O. Box 262550 • Baton Rouge, Louisiana 70826-2550
Website: www.jsm.org • Email: info@jsm.org
225-768-7000

TABLE OF CONTENTS

God's Plan For The Ages

The Cross Of Christ Series

God's Plan For The Ages

PART
ONE

THE ETERNAL
PAST

Chapter 1

The Eternal Triune God

CHAPTER ONE

THE ETERNAL TRIUNE GOD

"In the beginning God . . ." (Gen. 1:1).

GOD AS CREATOR

Mankind lives in a Universe whose vastness presupposes a Creator. But the question may arise, *"Who made the Creator?"* Science may continue regressing from cause to effect, but it cannot keep going back infinitely without acknowledging an Infinite Being. That Infinite Being is God, the Eternal One, the Cause and Source of every good thing that exists. God reveals Himself to man first as Creator:

"In the beginning GOD (Hebrew, *Elohim*) *created the heaven and the Earth"* (Gen. 1:1).

Human beings of every nation, tribe, and tongue acknowledge that there is a Supreme Being somewhere in the great beyond. Civilized and primitive men alike sense the need to worship something or someone. This need can be truly satisfied only by a worship encounter with the One True God. By Faith a person must believe that God is who He said He is:

"Without Faith it is impossible to please Him: for he who comes to God must believe that He is, and that He is a rewarder of them who diligently seek Him" (Heb. 11:6).

GOD AS *ELOHIM*

God has further revealed Himself to man as a plurality of perfect unity. Although the word *"Trinity"* is not found in the Scriptures, it does express the truth of God's revealed self. We worship God as Father, Son, and Holy Spirit because He has acknowledged Himself as such from the beginning. The Hebrew word *Elohim*, used in Genesis 1:1 and 2,700 other places in the Old Testament, is a uniplural noun meaning *"gods"* and is so translated 239 times (see Genesis 3:5; I Samuel 4:8; etc.). God as *Elohim* is not *One Person*, nor *one* in *number*, but *One* in perfect *unity*. There are three separate and distinct Persons in the Godhead known to us as Father, Son, and Holy Spirit, and yet these three are still One God:

"For there are Three Who bear record in Heaven, the Father, the Word, and the Holy Spirit: and these THREE are ONE" (I Jn. 5:7).

GOD AS A TRINITY

The only possible way that three of anything can be one is in the sense of unity. Even as a husband and a wife become ONE FLESH, through marriage, they still maintain their separate personalities and individuality. But in the sense of *unity*, they are not *two*, but *one*. A father, mother, and child, although they are three separate individuals, do not constitute THREE FAMILIES but only ONE FAMILY. Accordingly, we do *not* worship three Gods. We *do* worship three separate and distinct Persons, the Father, Jesus Christ, and the Holy Spirit, as ONE GOD — *ELOHIM*! In many cases in the Old Testament the triune God is indicated by the use of the plural pronoun *"us,"* such as in the following:

"And God (Elohim) said, Let US make man in OUR image, after OUR likeness" (Gen. 1:26).

IMAGE AND LIKENESS OF GOD

Here we have stated that all three Persons of the Godhead cooperated in the creation of man, and that man was created in the image and after the likeness of the triune God. This clearly teaches that each member of the Godhead has a personal Body, Soul, and Spirit. Adam was created not merely in the mental, moral, and spiritual image of God, but in the physical image as well — *"in our IMAGE, after our LIKENESS."*

Some persons have misinterpreted, *"God is a Spirit: and they who worship Him must worship Him in spirit and in truth"* (Jn. 4:24), to mean that God the Father does not have a bodily form, but is some kind of nebulous, ethereal substance unable to be seen. This simply is not so! Besides being unscriptural, it is ridiculous to think that throughout Eternity we would strive to relate to a Being so foreign to our existence. God has always desired to give a clear revelation of Himself to man and longs for a personal relationship with him.

PERSONAL BODY, SOUL, AND SPIRIT OF GOD

When the Bible states, *"God is a Spirit,"* the implication is that God has a spirit *Body*. The Apostle Paul understood this when he wrote:

"There is a natural body, and there is a spiritual body" (I Cor. 15:44).

Man also is a spirit (I Cor. 2:11; 5:3; 6:17; etc.), Paul declared, but has a natural body. When Jesus Christ walked the Earth 2,000 years ago, He was a Spirit in a natural body. After His Death and Resurrection, He possessed a spiritual *Body*, for He appeared to His Disciples and said:

"Behold My Hands and My Feet, that it is I Myself: handle Me,

and see; for a spirit has not flesh and bones, as you see Me have" (Lk. 24:39).

When the Disciples were fearful that they were seeing a ghost (Lk. 24:37), Jesus calmed their fears by revealing that He had a *spiritual Body* to which they could relate.

God the Father also has a spirit Body, for the Bible states:

"Then went up Moses, and Aaron, Nadab, and Abihu, and seventy of the Elders of Israel: And THEY SAW THE GOD OF ISRAEL: and there was under HIS FEET as it were a paved work of a Sapphire Stone, and as it were the body of Heaven in His clearness. And upon the nobles of the Children of Israel He laid not HIS HAND: also THEY SAW GOD, AND DID EAT AND DRINK. AND THE LORD said unto Moses, COME UP TO ME INTO THE MOUNT, AND BE THERE: AND I WILL GIVE YOU TABLES OF STONE . . ." (Ex. 24:9-12).

This clearly teaches that over 70 people saw God the Father prior to His giving the Law to Moses on Mount Sinai. It appears that God joined with them as they ate and drank together. Although it is evident that many of the appearances of the Lord in the Old Testament were theophanies of the preincarnate Christ, God the Father did appear to men on many occasions (Gen. 11:5-8; Ezek. 1:26-28; Acts 7:55-56; Rev. 5:1-7). The Bible also refers to the bodily parts of God. Moses saw the *"Back Parts"* of God (Ex. 33:18-23). God has a Heart (Gen. 6:6; 8:21), Hands and Fingers (Ex. 31:18; Ps. 8:3-6), Nostrils (Ps. 18:8), a Mouth (Num. 12:8), Lips and Tongue (Isa. 30:27), Feet (Ezek. 1:27), Eyes (Ps. 33:18); Hair, Head, Face, and Arms (Dan. 7:9-14; 10:5-19; Rev. 5:1-7; 22:4-6); and Ears (Isa. 59:1).

Although some persons would teach that the description of God with bodily parts is merely an anthropomorphism, the question must be answered, *"Why would God give us such descriptions if they were not true?"* Obviously enough, some descriptions of God must be taken figuratively (Ps. 91:4; Mal. 4:2), but we have no reason to spiritualize what may be taken literally.

Scriptures that state that God the Father cannot be seen (Jn. 1:18; 5:37) must be interpreted that God cannot be fully comprehended in all His Glory and Majesty by the natural mind. The Bible clearly teaches that many people have seen God. Although Moses was not allowed to see God's Face while on Mount Sinai (Ex. 33:20), we have the blessed Promise:

"And there shall be no more curse: but the Throne of GOD and of the LAMB shall be in it; and His servants shall serve Him: AND THEY SHALL SEE HIS FACE" (Rev. 22:3-4).

When we also have our glorified spiritual body, then we shall be able to have fellowship with God in all of His Glory and Splendor. What a day that will be! God is invisible (Col. 1:15) to us only in the sense that He dwells in Heaven, and we dwell on Earth. We cannot see Him now with the natural eye, but we can sense His Spirit, which is omnipresent.

Other Scriptures teaching a Divine Trinity are Genesis 11:5-7; Matthew 3:16-17; 28:19; Mark 12:35-37; John 1:1-2; 15:26; Acts 7:55-56; I John 5:7; and a host of others. A person will never fully understand the Godhead by theorizing that one person can be three persons. This is impossible; however, our One God is eternally existent in three Persons. Not One God with *three personalities* — that would make Him schizophrenic — but ONE GREAT GOD whom we worship and adore as Father, Son, and Holy Spirit.

DEITY OF OUR LORD JESUS CHRIST

The titles Son of God and Son of Man, when speaking of Jesus Christ, refer not to His Deity, but to His Humanity. He did not have a beginning AS GOD (Mic. 5:2; Jn. 1:1-2; Col. 1:17; etc.). Jesus Christ has ALWAYS BEEN GOD. He existed with the Father and the Holy Spirit for all of the eternal ages past. However, AS MAN He did have a beginning by being begotten of the Father through the Holy Spirit, and born of the Virgin Mary. Although Jesus was foreordained to be a Son (I Pet. 1:20), He did not become one until He was born in Bethlehem, fulfilling the Prophecy:

"I will declare the decree: the Lord has said unto Me, You are My Son; THIS DAY have I begotten You" (Ps. 2:7; Heb. 1:5; 5:5).

This is what the Angel had reference to when he told the shepherds:

"For unto you is born THIS DAY in the city of David a Saviour, which is Christ the Lord" (Lk. 2:11).

SONSHIP OF CHRIST

Therefore, Christ's Sonship refers not to His Deity but to His Humanity — *"God with us"* (Mat. 1:23).

So it is seen that in the eternal past there were always three distinct Persons in the Godhead, none of Whom was created, but was self-existent. In the Plan of God, it was predetermined that One would become the Father, that One would become the Son, and that One would become the Holy Spirit. This was realized in the Incarnation when Jesus was born the Son of God (Heb. 10:5; Mat. 1:23; Ps. 2:7; Lk. 1:35). It was in the eternal Plan of God for this to take place, to bring about our glorious Salvation through the offering of Jesus Christ, the Son of God — *"He shall save His people from their sins"* (Mat. 1:21).

GOD AS CREATOR OF THE HEAVENS

The eternal triune God has always existed, and has been at work throughout all the eternal past. After designing His Plan for all Eternity (Eph. 2:7; 3:5, 11; I Pet. 1:20), He called into existence the heavens, including the sun, moon, and stars (Gen. 1:1; Col. 1:15-18; Ps. 8:3; 90:2; 95:5; 102:25). This occurred somewhere in the dateless past, and will be discussed in a later chapter. God then created the Angelic Host along with the entire spirit world (Job 38:4-7; Col. 1:15-18). The spirit world as originally created included the following:

1. Angels (Heb. 1:14; Job 38:4-7);
2. Archangels (I Thess. 4:16; Jude, Vs. 9);
3. Cherubim (Gen. 3:24; Ezek. 10:5); and,
4. Seraphim (Isa. 6:1-3).

GOD AS CREATOR OF THE SPIRIT WORLD

Angels are described as *"ministering spirits"* (Heb. 1:14) and have filled this role down through the ages (I Ki. 19:5-7; Dan. 6:22; Mat. 4:11; Acts 12:5-10). Some of the Angels rule over particular nations of the Earth (Dan. 10:13-21; 12:1). They are also instrumental in carrying out God's orders (Gen. 19:1-25; II Ki. 19:35; Acts 12:23).

Archangels are in a class higher than common Angels; such as, Michael and Gabriel (Dan. 10:21; Lk. 1:19, 26; Jude, Vs. 9; Rev. 12:7-9).

Cherubim, it appears, are connected with God's retributive and redemptive purposes (Gen. 3:24; Ex. 25:22). Lucifer was created *"the anointed Cherub"* (Ezek. 28:14) and ruled on Earth.

Seraphim are mentioned in Isaiah, Chapter 6; other than that we know little about them. Their name means *"burning ones."*

All of the spirit world was created perfect and in harmony with God (Job 38:4-7; Ezek. 28:13-15). God enjoyed fellowship with the created Host of Heaven prior to His creating the original perfect Earth.

Chapter 2

The Original Perfect Earth

CHAPTER TWO

THE ORIGINAL PERFECT EARTH

"In the beginning God created the heaven and the Earth" (Gen. 1:1).

DESCRIPTION IN GENESIS 1:1

This is God's first and final reply to the questions that have intrigued mankind concerning the origin of the Universe in the dateless past. If a person can accept the First Verse of the Bible, he will have no problem believing the rest of the Book! God makes no apologies for this statement — *"In the beginning God created."* He does not stoop to explain HOW He did it, or even WHY He did it. A person must either accept it or reject it. Faith is essential to a thorough understanding of God's creative Plan.

"Through Faith we understand that the worlds (Greek, *aion, ages*) *were framed by the Word of God, so that things which are seen were not made of things which do appear"* (Heb. 11:3).

IN THE BEGINNING

Genesis 1:1 is speaking of the original perfect Earth, for we know that everything God designs is perfect (Deut. 32:4; Ps. 18:30; James 1:17). God's original Creation was not as the next verse describes, *"without form, and void."* The Creation of Genesis 1:1 was flawlessly perfect, but in the very next verse we find a ruined creation, in chaos and disorder, as the result of some great cataclysmic catastrophe. It is described:

"And that Earth was without form, and void; and darkness was upon the face of the deep" (Gen. 1:2).

NOT A CHAOTIC STATE

The Prophet Isaiah clearly taught that the original Earth was NOT created *"without form, and void"*:

"For thus saith the LORD Who created the heavens; God Himself Who formed the Earth and made it; He has established it, HE CREATED IT NOT IN VAIN (Hebrew, *tohu,* empty, desolate), *He formed it to be inhabited: I am the LORD; and there is none else"* (Isa. 45:18).

AN INHABITABLE STATE

The Revised Standard Version of the Bible translates this, *"He did not create it a CHAOS."* Isaiah also stated that the original perfect Earth was created in a habitable state. Just who the inhabitants were will be discussed later.

The above Scriptures and a host of others clearly reveal that God created the original perfect Earth, prior to Adam, somewhere in the dateless past — *"in the beginning."* Exactly how long ago this took place nobody knows. Scientists tell us that the world is probably several millions or even billions of years old. A thorough understanding of the Word of God reveals that there is no contradiction between what the scientists tell us and what the Bible declares.

SCIENCE VS. BIBLE

The problem has been that some theologians have misinterpreted many Scriptures dealing with Creation. They have made such statements as: *"The Earth is approximately 6,000 years old."* *"Dinosaurs and other prehistoric animals were contemporaries with Adam, Enoch, and Noah."* Science has proven these opinions utterly ridiculous! Unfortunately, many scientists who hear such remarks do not question the words of theologians, but question the Bible itself! *This should not be!* The Word of God reveals the Truth of God. Although our feeble handling of Scripture may be in error, the Bible is ALWAYS right on target! And the fact of the matter is that many scientists and archaeologists, the world over, are discovering that when their findings seemingly contradict the Bible, always in a matter of time, after further scientific scrutiny, *the Word of God proves to be true!*

Between the First and Second Verses of Genesis, Chapter One, which speak of *the original perfect Earth,* and between the Second and Third Verses, which speak of *the chaotic Earth,* the Biblical account of Creation leaves two great white pages, on which scientists may write what they will, in order to fill up the blanks of natural history. Of both of these cartes blanches, revelation has given only a superscription, a summary table of contents. The first runs, *"In the beginning God created the heaven and the Earth."* How this was, how long it lasted, what followed thereon, what changes and revolutions took place, down to the state of things described in the chaotic Earth of Verse Two, the Scriptures give us only a glimpse.

The second carte blanche has the summary inscription, *"The Earth was without form, and void; and darkness was upon the face of the deep. And the Spirit of God moved upon the face of the waters."* What influence the Holy Spirit brooding over the waters had upon the chaotic Earth, what operations and formations He called forth in them, the Bible does not fully give. Scientists have attempted to fill up this void between the original perfect Earth and the chaotic Earth, and some of their efforts are commendable. The Word of God, however, for the most part, neither substantiates nor repudiates their discoveries.

GENESIS 1:1 AND 1:2 — TWO SEPARATE ACCOUNTS

What are the other evidences in Scripture that Genesis 1:1 speaks of the original perfect Earth and Genesis 1:2 describes the chaotic Earth prior to the six days of the Creation of the present Earth? In the Masoretic text of Genesis, in which ancient Jewish scholars attempted to incorporate a sufficient number of *"indicators"* to assist the reader in correct pronunciation and interpretation of the text, there is a small mark known as a *rebhia* following Verse One. This mark is a disjunctive accent, which serves to inform the reader that there is a break in the narrative at this point, and that he should pause before going on to the next verse, which speaks of the chaotic Earth.

BARA VS. ASAH

God created the original perfect Earth *ex nihilo* (Isa. 45:18), meaning *"out of nothing."* The word *"created"* in Genesis 1:1 comes from the Hebrew word *bara*, which means *"to create, to bring into being"* without the use of preexisting materials. The present Earth was not created in this sense, for the Hebrew word used is *asah*, which means *"to make out of already existing materials."* Therefore, the original perfect Earth was *"created" (bara)* in the beginning, passed into a chaotic state for reasons we shall later discover, and the present Earth was *"made" (asah)* in six literal 24-hour days as the Bible plainly teaches:

"For in six days the LORD made [asah] heaven and Earth, the sea, and all that in them is, and rested the seventh day . . ." (Ex. 20:11).

In considering the phrase *"And the Earth was without form, and void,"* there are good reasons for thinking that *"but"* would be a better translation of the first word than *"and,"* so that the phrase would read, *"BUT the Earth was without form, and void."*

1. The conjunctions *"and"* and *"but"* are not distinguished in Hebrew. The word is *waw*. The Greek equivalent is *kai*.

2. The most ancient Hebrews themselves, who were well exercised in and conversant with the peculiarities of their native tongue, interpreted it by

the disjunctive participle *"but,"* and *none* of them by the copulative *"and."*

3. It was rendered thus by the first interpreters of the text, the Jews of Alexandria, nearly 300 years before the Christian era.

4. Josephus, the learned Jewish historian, paraphrased the Passage in this manner.

5. In the same manner, the Chaldean paraphrase, the Targum of Onkelos, renders it in the Latin, *"the Earth, HOWEVER, was. . . ."*

6. The old Latin Version and the Vulgate, translated by Jerome from the original Hebrew with the aid of the other translations of his time, translates it thus.

7. The early Church Fathers, including Tertullian and Clement, translate this as *"but"* instead of *"and."*

The word *"was"* in this phrase is the Hebrew word *hayah,* which is a verb *"to become,"* not the verb *"to be."* The phrase should actually be translated, *"BUT the Earth HAD BECOME without form, and void,"* for the word *hayah* is rendered *"became"* 67 times, such as *"Man BECAME a living soul"* (Gen. 2:7; compare Gen. 19:26; 20:12; 24:67; Ex. 4:3; *et al*). *Hayah* is also translated *"becamest," "came to pass," "become," "come to pass,"* and many times *"be"* in the sense of *"become"* (Gen. 1:3; 3:5; etc.).

Therefore, a proper understanding of the translation of Genesis 1:1-2 proves that God did not originally create the Earth in such a wasted and ruined state. If the Earth was not originally created *"without form, and void,"* as we have seen from Isaiah 45:18, then it must have been created, inhabited, and later BECAME desolate. How this occurred will be discussed after further consideration of the original perfect Earth.

PRESENCE OF ANGELS AT EARTH'S CREATION

God beautifully described the Creation of the original perfect Earth in the Book of Job:

"Where were you when I laid the foundations of the Earth? declare, if you have understanding. Who has laid the measures thereof, if you know? or who has stretched the line upon it? Whereupon are the foundations thereof fastened? or who laid the corner stone thereof; When the morning stars sang together, and all the sons of God shouted for joy?" (Job 38:4-7).

The *"morning stars"* referred to in this Passage are the infinite stars out in space, which are suns to other Planets like our sun is to Earth and its related Planets. This explains the fact that the heavens were created prior to the creation of Planet Earth:

"The heavens declare the Glory of God; and the firmament shows

His handywork" (Ps. 19:1).

It is in this sense that the stars *"sang together."* The *"sons of God"* mentioned in these Scriptures can be none other than the mighty Angelic Host created by God *before* He created the original perfect Earth. Lucifer also was numbered with the Angels who were created in beauty and perfection. He is called the *"son of the morning"* (Isa. 14:12). The name Lucifer actually means *"light-bearing."* He was created perfect. He was not created as the Devil or the Evil One.

LUCIFER, RULER OF EARTH IN HIS PERFECTED STATE

The Prophet Ezekiel referred to Lucifer in Chapter 28 when he was addressing the king of Tyre. This is the hermeneutical principle of Biblical Interpretation called the law of double reference. God was speaking to the earthly king of Tyre, but much of what He stated could in no wise be attributed to any human being. We see another example of the law of double reference in the New Testament:

"But He (Jesus) *turned, and said unto Peter, Get thee behind Me, Satan: you are an offence unto Me: for you savor not the things that be of God, but those that be of men"* (Mat. 16:23).

Now, obviously, the Apostle Peter was not the Devil. Jesus merely looked beyond Peter and addressed Satan who was inspiring the words that Peter spoke. It was in this same sense that the Lord addressed the king of Tyre when He was actually speaking to Lucifer:

"Thus saith the Lord GOD; You seal up the sum, full of wisdom, and perfect in beauty. You have been in Eden the Garden of God; every precious stone was your covering, the sardius, topaz, and the diamond, the beryl, the onyx, and the jasper, the sapphire, the emerald, and the carbuncle, and gold: the workmanship of your tabrets and of your pipes was prepared in you in the day that you were created. You are the anointed Cherub who covers; and I have set you so: you were upon the Holy Mountain of God; you have walked up and down in the midst of the stones of fire. You were perfect in your ways from the day that you were created, till iniquity was found in you" (Ezek. 28:12-15).

Here we find some interesting statements concerning Lucifer and his relationship to the original perfect Earth:

1. Lucifer was full of wisdom, and an extremely intelligent being.
2. He was absolutely beautiful.
3. He was a created being.
4. He was *"the anointed Cherub that covers."* Lucifer was an Angel empowered by the Spirit of God to protect and overshadow the

Creation of God.

5.　He was set or appointed by God to rule the original perfect Earth.

6.　Lucifer dwelled in the Garden of Eden in a beautiful and perfected state long before Adam and Eve.　The original perfect Earth had such a Garden, as did the present Earth.　The Garden of Eden in the original perfect Earth, it seems, was even more beautiful than Adam's Eden, as evidenced by the many precious stones and gems that were Lucifer's covering in the Garden.

7.　The Mountain of God was the place where Lucifer had his kingdom.　This was on the Earth, as other Scriptures teach.

8.　He was perfect in all his ways, in total obedience to God.

This Passage plainly declares that Lucifer in his perfected, created state lived on the original perfect Earth in the Garden of Eden appointed by God to rule the Planet.　The Earth, at this time, must have been a beautiful place!　We are given only a glimpse of its majestic magnitude.　How long Lucifer ruled and reigned under God's appointment is not known.　Not until we begin our study of the chaotic Earth shall we gain a greater insight into this original Creation of God and Lucifer's involvement in bringing its beauty and perfection to an end.

Chapter 3

The Chaotic Earth

CHAPTER THREE

THE CHAOTIC EARTH

"And the Earth was without form, and void; and darkness was upon the face of the deep. And the Spirit of God moved upon the face of the waters" (Gen. 1:2).

DESCRIPTION IN GENESIS 1:2

As has already been proved, a better translation of this Verse would be, *"BUT the Earth HAD BECOME without form, and void,"* thus explaining the fact that the original perfect Earth was not created *"without form, and void,"* as Isaiah 45:18 plainly teaches, but passed into this condition at a later time.

DESCRIPTION BY JEREMIAH

The Prophet Jeremiah gave another view of the original perfect Earth in its chaotic state prior to Adam. In this Passage, God's purpose in showing Jeremiah the past desolation of the Earth was to teach Israel that her land was to be desolate because of rebellion, but not totally destroyed as was the Earth in its chaotic condition.

"I beheld the Earth, and, lo, it was without form, and void; and the heavens, and they had no light. I beheld the mountains, and, lo, they trembled, and all the hills moved lightly. I beheld, and, lo, there was no man, and all the birds of the heavens were fled. I beheld, and, lo, the fruitful place was a wilderness, and all the cities thereof were broken down at the Presence of the LORD, and by His fierce anger" (Jer. 4:23-26).

TOHU WA BOHU — WITHOUT FORM, AND VOID

The phrase, *"Without form, and void"* (Hebrew, *tohu wa bohu*) in the above Passage is used identically in Genesis 1:2 with reference to the chaotic Earth. From the outset we can say unequivocally that both words, *tohu* and *bohu*, whether occurring together or separately, are used throughout the Bible to describe something under the Judgment of God. *Tohu* is used of something that has been laid waste (Isa. 24:10; 34:11; Jer. 4:23) or has become a desert (Deut. 32:10) or is idolatrous and therefore displeasing to God (Isa. 41:29). With the Hebrew preposition *lamedth*

27

it becomes an adverb (Isa. 49:4) and means *"wastefully"* or *"in vain."* In Isaiah 45:18, which we have already considered, the Prophet said specifically that God did not create the Earth in a state of *tohu.* Whether we interpret the *tohu* of this Passage to mean simply *"a desolation"* or to mean *"in vain"* is of little importance; the suggestion is the same.

What caused the Earth to pass into this chaotic state Jeremiah described? Before we answer that question, let us consider further the Prophet's view of the original perfect Earth (Jer., Chpt. 4):

1. There were mountains and hills (Vs. 24);
2. There were fruitful places, gardens, etc. (Vs. 26);
3. There were cities (Vs. 26);
4. There were birds, animals, etc. (Vs. 25);
5. There were men who lived in the cities; but these cities were broken down; all vegetation, men, and animals were totally destroyed by the Presence of the Lord and by His fierce anger (Vs. 25);
6. The Earth had become *tohu wa bohu* (Vs. 23); and,
7. The heavens were withholding their light (Vs. 23).

This gives us a panoramic view of the chaotic Earth mentioned in Genesis 1:2 and explains why *"darkness was upon the face of the deep."* Jeremiah stated that the mountains and hills of the original perfect Earth were shaken with an earthquake, which no doubt caused the remains of animals, dinosaurs, prehistoric men, etc., to be deposited in the depths of the Earth beneath many layers of solid rock, such as are now being found by scientists and archaeologists.

REIGN OF LUCIFER ON THE EARTH

We already have discovered that Lucifer was given dominion over the original perfect Earth. The Prophet Isaiah also confirmed this and gave the account of his fall:

"How are you fallen from Heaven, O Lucifer, son of the morning! How are you cut down to the ground, which did weaken the nations! For you have said in your heart, I will ascend into Heaven, I will exalt my throne above the stars of God: I will sit also upon the mount of the congregation, in the sides of the north: I will ascend above the heights of the clouds; I will be like the Most High" (Isa. 14:12-14).

REBELLION OF LUCIFER AND EARTH'S INHABITANTS

From this Passage we discover that although he was created a perfect Angelic being, *"the anointed Cherub that covers"* (Ezek. 28:14), Lucifer coveted the glory and power that belonged only to

God. Because of pride he led a rebellion against God and suffered the Judgment of God.

Notice that it is stated that Lucifer *"weaken*(ed) *the nations"* of the Earth. Not only did Lucifer persuade one-third of the Angelic Host to rebel with him, but he also convinced the inhabitants of the original perfect Earth, the *"cities"* of men that Jeremiah saw, and the *"nations"* that Isaiah described, to join his forces. The Angels mentioned in Revelation 12:4 and the inhabitants of the original perfect Earth sided with Lucifer against Almighty God!

Notice also that Lucifer wanted to exalt his throne (denoting his rulership and authority) *"above"* the stars of God. He wanted to ascend *"above"* the heights of the clouds.

Isaiah proved that Lucifer's kingdom was the original perfect Earth, and that his subjects were the inhabitants of the Earth that Jeremiah described in Chapter Four of his Prophecy. It also should be recalled that Isaiah 45:18 clearly taught that God created the original perfect Earth *"to be inhabited."*

DISTINCTION BETWEEN DEMONS AND FALLEN ANGELS

Many Bible scholars teach that demons (which are to be distinguished from fallen Angels) are the disembodied spirits of this pre-Adamite race. There are many reasons for holding to this view:

1. Angels have their own spirit bodies. We never read in Scripture of Angels seeking to possess humans.

2. Demons are disembodied spirits and are constantly seeking to possess humans (Mat. 12:43-45).

3. Demons, on one occasion, besought Jesus, *"that he would not send them away out of the country"* (Mk. 5:10). Jesus granted their wish. It seems that demons desire to stay in certain localities which may have been the scene of their sins on the original perfect Earth.

4. Their efforts to re-embody themselves in human beings is looked upon as evidence that they once possessed bodies similar to humans.

It seems only logical that demons are the spirits of those who trod the original perfect Earth in the flesh. How long they existed with Lucifer in this perfect environment simply is not revealed in the Bible.

However, at the time of the great destruction of the original perfect Earth described in Genesis 1:2, the pre-Adamites were destroyed by God, their spirit was disembodied and left still under the power, ultimately to share the fate of the leader in whose sin they acquiesced — Lucifer. Although the prehistoric bodies scientists have discovered may be evidence of a pre-Adamite race, it also may be that God judged them by reducing them in a moment to *"ashes upon the Earth"* (Ezek. 28:18).

It may be that the Earth opened her mouth and swallowed them up, with all that appertained to them, so that they went *"down* (alive) *into the pit,"* as did Korah and his rebels (Num. 16:30). It also may be that the pre-Adamites perished in what is now to us the deep, and that their remains are covered by the deposit at the bottom of the ocean.

The Bible does not give a full account of this civilization simply because the Word of God is not written as a history of Angels or other beings. It is a written history of God's dealing with mankind in this present Earth on which we now live.

CAUSE AND EFFECT OF LUCIFER'S FALL

What was the cause of Lucifer's fall? Obviously enough, it was his rebellion against the Plan of God for the original perfect Earth. He sought to be worshiped and esteemed above the Almighty. His fall was brought about as a result of pride:

"Your heart was lifted up because of your beauty, you have corrupted your wisdom by reason of your brightness" (Ezek. 28:17).

The demise of Lucifer is a constant reminder to all that *"pride goes before destruction, and an haughty spirit before a fall"* (Prov. 16:18). Jesus in referring to the rebellion and casting out of Lucifer stated, *"I beheld Satan as lightning fall from Heaven"* (Lk. 10:18).

DESTRUCTION OF THE EARTH BY A FLOOD

How long God allowed Lucifer and his subjects to remain upon the original perfect Earth in their fallen state is not known. It may have been a short time, or it could have been many thousands of years, even as God has allowed sinful man to continue on the present Earth for some 6,000 years.

What we *do* know is that God brought the original perfect Earth to its end by means of a universal flood, which destroyed every man, animal, and plant (Jer. 4:25-26) and left the Earth in a chaotic state. This explains the *"water"* over which the Holy Spirit brooded in Genesis 1:2, as previously mentioned.

The Apostle Peter gave us some insight into the destruction of the original perfect Earth:

"There shall come in the last days scoffers, walking after their own lusts, And saying, Where is the Promise of His Coming? For since the fathers fell asleep, all things continue AS THEY WERE FROM THE BEGINNING OF THE CREATION. For this they willingly are

ignorant of, that by the Word of God the Heavens were of old, and the Earth standing out of the water and in the water: Whereby the world THAT THEN WAS, being overflowed with water, perished: But the Heavens and the Earth, WHICH ARE NOW, by the same Word are kept in store, reserved unto fire against the Day of Judgment and Perdition of ungodly men" (II Pet. 3:3-7).

END OF THE WORLD THAT THEN WAS

Peter clearly taught that there was a civilization on the Earth prior to Adam, which he called *"the world that then was."* He was referring, of course, to the original perfect Earth that God destroyed with water. He then spoke of *"the Heavens and the Earth, which are now,"* referring to this present Earth that one day will be renovated by fire. Earth already has had a *"water"* baptism (Gen. 1:2) and will, at the end of the Millennium, experience a *"fire"* baptism (II Pet. 3:7). After the present Earth is renovated by fire, Peter went on to say:

"Nevertheless we, according to His Promise, look for new Heavens and A NEW EARTH, wherein dwells Righteousness" (II Pet. 3:13).

God will not suffer defeat in His program! It may appear that not only did Satan defeat God's program for the original perfect Earth, but he also defeated God's Plan for the present Earth. But, take heart, we are looking for *"a new Earth"* where God Himself shall *"dwell with"* His people (Rev. 21:3).

How do we know that Peter was not referring to the flood in Noah's day?

1. The context is *"the beginning of the creation."*

2. The *"world* (Greek, *kosmos,* social system) *that then was"* perished. The civilization did not perish in Noah's day, but was perpetuated by himself and his three sons.

3. Noah's flood merely drowned the Earth. There was not a re-creation of the Earth following that Deluge, as in *"the Heavens and the Earth, which are now."*

Not only does II Peter 3:3-7 prove that the original perfect Earth was destroyed by a great cataclysmic flood, but also Genesis 1:2; Jeremiah 4:23-26; and Psalm 104:5-7.

"Who laid the foundations of the Earth, that it should not be removed for ever. You cover it with the deep as with a garment: the waters stood above the mountains. At Your rebuke they fled; at the voice of Your thunder they hasted away" (Ps. 104:5-7).

The flood that destroyed the original perfect Earth covered the entire Planet, even the tops of the mountains. How long the Earth remained in this chaotic state the Bible does not say. We do know, however, both from the Scriptures and from science that the Earth went through a great catastrophe at an unknown period in the past. Animal remains show that they died in great agony and suddenly.

There are scores of questions that will go unanswered without a proper understanding of the original perfect Earth, its chaotic state, and the six days of re-creation of the present Earth. Although the Bible, as mentioned already, gives us only a brief overview of this mysterious beginning, we are supplied enough information to understand the origin of the Universe. Putting it all in brief summary:

1. God created the heavens and the Earth, in the beginning, in the dateless past (Gen. 1:1; Job 38:4-7).

2. He allowed the heavens and the Earth to be inhabited and appointed Lucifer over the Earth (Col. 1:15-18; Rev. 12:4).

3. Lucifer ruled for God on the Earth for an unknown span of time and then rebelled, invading Heaven to dethrone God (Ezek. 28:11-18; Isa. 14:12-14).

4. Lucifer and his followers were defeated, and the Earth was destroyed by a flood and by the fierce anger of God (Gen. 1:2; Jer. 4:23-26; Ps. 104:5-9; II Pet. 3:5-6).

5. The flood stayed on the Earth for an unknown time (Gen. 1:2).

Following this chaotic condition, however long this may have been, God restored the Earth in six literal 24-hour days, and made Adam and his Creation to carry out God's Plan upon the present Earth.

Chapter 4

The Present Earth

CHAPTER FOUR

THE PRESENT EARTH

"And God said, Let there be light: and there was light. And God saw the light, that it was good: and God divided the light from the darkness. And God called the light Day, and the darkness He called Night. And the evening and the morning were the first day" (Gen. 1:3-5).

DESCRIPTION IN GENESIS 1:3-31

It already has been proved that the First Verse of Genesis, Chapter 1 declares the Creation of the original heavens and the Earth. The Second Verse describes the Earth as being wasted and void. Now we come to the Third Verse, which reveals God beginning the work of renewing the desolate and chaotic Earth so that His Divine Plan for mankind can be accomplished. It is interesting to note how Genesis 1:2-5 gives us insight into the nature of God and the love He possesses for His Creation.

ORDER OUT OF CHAOS

The Prophet Isaiah gave us the picture of God creating a perfect and orderly world (Isa. 45:18). Besides the other proofs that have been given showing the fact that God did not create the Earth in chaos and disorder, a sensible view of the Heart of God also will be evidence of this. Everything that God creates is perfect (Gen. 1:31; Isa. 45:18; James 1:17). God never has created something in chaos and disorder! Satan, however, is the master of this! He loves to turn what God has made good into that which is bad, that which is holy into that which is profane, that which is orderly into a total chaos. The Devil delights in corrupting the life and twisting the mind of men and women. Jesus said:

"The thief comes not, but for to steal, and to kill, and to destroy: I am come that they might have life, and that they might have it more abundantly" (Jn. 10:10).

Even as Satan took great pleasure in rendering the Creation of God a total shambles, he also delights in doing this to the heart of people. But God, through the marvelous work of His Divine Grace is able, in a moment's time, to restore that which the Devil has brought into chaos, and make it more beautiful than before! God longs to do this in the heart of those who will let Him! The drunkard, the prostitute, the drug addict whose mind is totally destroyed can be transformed from a life of chaos and destruction into a life of joy and peace!

Notice also that Genesis 1:3 states that God called the light out of darkness. God cannot be associated with darkness, nor could his original Creation have been such:

"This then is the Message which we have heard of Him, and declare unto you, that GOD IS LIGHT AND IN HIM IS NO DARKNESS AT ALL" (I Jn. 1:5).

Even as we know that the chaos and disorder that plagued the Earth came from Satan, we also know that the *"darkness . . . upon the face of the deep"* was associated with his fall. And it is true also in the life of those under Satan's control — they are full of darkness:

"But if your eye be evil, your whole body shall be full of darkness" (Mat. 6:23).

Jesus stated that *"men* (love) *darkness rather than light, because their deeds* (are) *evil"* (Jn. 3:19). Although Satan desires to transform himself into *"an angel of light"* (II Cor. 11:14), he is only a counterfeit! The entire kingdom of Satan is full of darkness (Eph. 6:12; Col. 1:13), but the Kingdom of God is full of Light (I Pet. 2:9; I Jn. 1:7). Although Satan would love to spread his darkness throughout the entire Earth again as he once did, the Light of the Gospel is being preached literally around the world! And everyone who obeys the Gospel, regardless of how full of sin and darkness he may be, can experience the life-changing Power of God:

"Giving thanks unto the Father, which has made us meet to be partakers of the inheritance of the Saints in Light: WHO HAS DELIVERED US FROM THE POWER OF DARKNESS, AND HAS TRANSLATED US INTO THE KINGDOM OF HIS DEAR SON" (Col. 1:12-13).

Therefore, we understand that Satan always turns order into chaos and light into darkness, but God always transforms darkness into light and chaos into order! Genesis 1:5 gives us further insight into God's Plan for man:

"And the evening and the morning were the first day" (Gen. 1:5).

EVENING AND MORNING

We normally think of a day as *morning to evening.* In God's timing, however, the order is *evening to morning!* In life, there are many experiences that cause men and women to go through what, it seems, is the darkest night — the discovery of a terminal illness, the loss of a loved one. It is during such times of grief and sorrow that God is able to prove His great Love! When it seems that all is dark, and the sun never will shine again,

God always shows His faithfulness to His Children:

"Weeping may endure for a night, but joy comes in the morning" (Ps. 30:5).

During times of heartache and sorrow, we can lean on the Lord and thank Him for His Promises! What Satan turns to darkness, God will transform into light. And when Satan would try to bring a tragedy in the darkness of night, God always gives the glorious promise of a new day!

SIX LITERAL TWENTY-FOUR HOUR DAYS

It clearly is recorded that God restored the Earth to a habitable state in six literal 24-hour days (Gen. 1:3-31). The six days of Creation were not geological ages or periods of time. There could have been eons of ages that lapsed upon the Earth between Genesis 1:1 and 1:2, as already discussed; but when God reestablished the Earth, He did so in six solar days:

"For IN SIX DAYS the LORD made (Hebrew, *asah,* made, not created) *heaven and Earth, the sea, and all that in them is, and rested the seventh day"* (Ex. 20:11).

In this Verse Moses likened the six workdays of man to the six days in which the Lord renewed that chaotic Earth. There is no reason to view the days of Creation as periods of time anymore than there is reason to refer to the six workdays of man as six periods of time.

Some persons have misconstrued the Scripture verse . . . *"One day is with the Lord as a thousand years, and a thousand years as one day"* (II Pet. 3:8) . . . to state that the six days of Creation are to be understood as ages of time. However, God says not that one day IS a thousand years, but that one day is AS a thousand years, as far as time is concerned. The eternal God is not concerned with any particular span of time, for compared to eternity, time is immaterial. It is true that the word *"day"* is used in Scripture to refer to an extended period of time such as, *"the day of the Lord"* (II Pet. 3:10); but in Genesis, Chapter 1 each day is limited to *"the evening and the morning"* and is numbered individually. We have no reason not to take literally what God has so simply stated in His Word.

As the six days of Creation are studied, the two Hebrew words *bara, "create,"* and *asah, "made,"* must be redefined, for they are two distinctly different words in the Hebrew text. The word *bara, "create,"* has to do with the divine action of bringing into existence that which did not already exist and is used only three times in Genesis, Chapter 1. However, the word *asah, "made,"* is used in the remainder of the Chapter.

On the first day God did not *create* the light; He *made it to appear* (1:3). On the second day God did not *create* the waters (for they already existed), but *divided* the waters (1:6). On the third day God did not *create* the Earth (for it was created *"in the beginning"*), but made the dry land to *appear* from beneath the waters (1:9). On the fourth day God did not *create* the sun, moon, and stars; He *regulated* the already existing solar system (1:14-18).

However, the word *bara*, *"create,"* that is used in Genesis 1:1, with reference to the original Creation, *"in the beginning,"* is used also in connection with the creation of animal life (1:21). Because life was again being introduced, the creative Power of God was essential during the fifth and sixth days of re-creation, as it was *"in the beginning."*

When God began to reestablish the Earth, the entire globe was covered with water, and the Spirit of God was hovering over the surface (Gen. 1:2).

THE FIRST DAY
"And God said, Let there be light: and there was light. And God saw the light, that it was good: and God divided the light from the darkness. And God called the light Day, and the darkness He called Night. And the evening and the morning were the first day" (Gen. 1:3-5).

DAY I — RESTORATION OF LIGHT

The events of the first day restored light to the Planet and regulated day and night on the Earth as it was originally in the beginning (Jer. 4:23-26). There was a time when scientists questioned the Genesis account of Creation because it recorded light existing apparently before the Creation of the sun. It since has been proved that cosmic light can exist on the Earth apart from the sun, and under certain conditions the Earth may become self-luminous.

THE SECOND DAY
"And God said, Let there be a firmament in the midst of the waters, and let it divide the waters from the waters. And God made the firmament, and divided the waters which were under the firmament from the waters which were above the firmament: and it was so. And God called the firmament heaven. And the evening and the morning were the second day" (Gen. 1:6-8).

DAY II — RESTORATION OF ATMOSPHERE

There are three *"heavens"* referred to in Scripture: the first heaven, or the clouds (Ps. 77:17-18; 104:2, 3); the second heaven, or the starry space (Isa. 13:10; 14:13); and the third Heaven where God dwells (Isa.

14:12-14; II Cor. 12:2-4). The firmament described in this Passage is the first heaven — the clouds, which were originally created to retain moisture to water the Earth (Isa. 14:12-14; Job 38:25-30; Ps. 104:2-3). God simply restored the atmosphere to its original condition by raising part of the waters that covered the Earth into the clouds. Therefore, the atmosphere providing oxygen for the sustenance of life was established.

There is a significant omission from the record of this day's work, for the words of approval, *"and God saw that it was good,"* are not stated in connection with the atmosphere. In all likelihood, as soon as the firmament was established, the disembodied spirits of the pre-Adamic world along with Lucifer, *"the prince of the powers of the AIR"* (Eph. 2:2), swarmed into the Earth's atmosphere.

THE THIRD DAY
"And God said, Let the waters under the heaven be gathered together unto one place, and let the dry land appear: and it was so. And God called the dry land Earth; and the gathering together of the waters called He Seas: and God saw that it was good. And God said, Let the Earth bring forth grass, the herb yielding seed, and the fruit tree yielding fruit after his kind, whose seed is in itself, upon the Earth: and it was so. And the Earth brought forth grass, and herb yielding seed after his kind, and the tree yielding fruit, whose seed was in itself, after his kind: and God saw that it was good. And the evening and the morning were the third day" (Gen. 1:9-13).

DAY III — RESTORATION OF LAND AND VEGETATION

After the firmament was completed, God spoke again and the whole Planet resounded with the roar of rushing floods as they hastened from the dry land into places God has prepared for them, and the mountains and valleys reappeared:

"Who laid the foundations of the Earth, that it should not be removed for ever. You cover it with the deep as with a garment: THE WATERS STOOD ABOVE THE MOUNTAINS. AT YOUR REBUKE THEY FLED; AT THE VOICE OF YOUR THUNDER THEY HASTED AWAY. THEY GO UP BY THE MOUNTAINS; THEY GO DOWN BY THE VALLEYS UNTO THE PLACE WHICH YOU HAVE FOUNDED FOR THEM. You have set a bound that they may not pass over; that they turn not again to cover the Earth" (Ps. 104:5-9).

As recalled, the work of this day was not an original act, for there were mountains and valleys on the Earth prior to the third day (Ezek. 28:14; Jer. 4:23-26). Hence, the water of Genesis 1:2 covered the pre-Adamic Earth, along with the fossil deposits of a prior civilization. That is the reason that God merely commanded, *"Let the dry land APPEAR: and it was so."* It had long since before been *created.*

Also, on the third day, God restored the vegetation of the Earth and set in motion the process of reproduction *"after his kind."* This excludes the process of evolution during the six days of re-creation. Thus, the Earth was completely restored and again fitted for the support and enjoyment of life.

THE FOURTH DAY

"And God said, Let their be lights in the firmament of the heaven to divide the day from the night; and let them be for signs, and for seasons, and for days, and years: And let them be for lights in the firmament of the heaven to give light upon the Earth: and it was so. And God made two great lights; the greater light to rule the day, and the lesser light to rule the night: He made the stars also. And God set them in the firmament of the heaven to give light upon the Earth. And to rule over the day and over the night, and to divide the light from the darkness: and God saw that it was good. And the evening and the morning were the fourth day" (Gen. 1:14-19).

DAY IV — REGULATION OF SOLAR SYSTEM

The fourth day brought about the regulation of the solar system to give light on the Earth and to regulate the times and the seasons. It is not said that God created the sun, moon, and stars on the fourth day, but merely that He made or appointed them. They were created *"in the beginning,"* but withheld their light due to the Judgment of God on the pre-Adamic Earth (Gen. 1:2; Jer. 4:23).

THE FIFTH DAY

"And God said, Let the waters bring forth abundantly the moving creature that has life, and fowl that may fly above the Earth in the open firmament of heaven. And God created great whales, and every living creature that moves, which the waters brought forth abundantly, after their kind, and every winged fowl after his kind: and God saw that is was good. And God blessed them, saying, Be fruitful, and mul-tiply, and fill the waters in the seas, and let fowl multiply in the Earth. And the evening and the morning were the fifth day" (Gen. 1:20-23).

DAY V — CREATION OF FISH AND FOWL

For the first time since Genesis 1:1 the word *bara* is used again in reference to an original creative act. Due to the fact that all animals had been destroyed in Lucifer's flood, God created new fish for the waters and fowl for the air. Each creature was commanded to reproduce *"after his kind."* This, too, leaves no room for evolution to occur outside of a particular species.

THE SIXTH DAY

"And God said, Let the Earth bring forth the living creature after his kind, cattle, and creeping thing, and beast of the Earth after his kind: and it was so. And God made the beast of the Earth after his kind, and cattle after their kind, and every thing that creeps upon the Earth after his kind: and God saw that it was good. And God said, Let Us make man in Our Image, after Our Likeness: and let them have dominion over the fish of the sea, and over the fowl of the air, and over the cattle, and over all the Earth, and over every creeping thing that creeps upon the Earth. So God created man in His Own Image, in the Image of God created He him; male and female created He them. And God blessed them, and God said unto them, Be fruitful, and multiply, and replenish the Earth, and subdue it: and have dominion over the fish of the sea, and over the fowl of the air, and over every living thing that moves upon the Earth. . . . And God saw every thing that He had made, and, behold, it was very good. And the evening and the morning were the sixth day" (Gen. 1:24-31).

DAY VI — CREATION OF ANIMALS AND MAN

On the sixth day God created new land animals and commanded them to produce *"after their kind."* The evolutionary process does not extend beyond a particular species according to the provision of God. The fact remains today; for instance, a donkey and a mare when crossed produce a mule, which is sterile. God placed this reproductive law into effect during the sixth day of re-creation. The animal kingdom originally was not created carnivorous, but ate the green herb of the field only (Gen. 1:30). This will be the case once again, when the curse is lifted from the Earth and the meat-eating appetite of the animal kingdom once again will be eradicated (Isa. 11:6-7).

DISTINCTION BETWEEN GENESIS 1 AND 2 ACCOUNTS

Some persons have understood Genesis 1:24-31 and 2:5-25 to refer to two separate Creation accounts. It should be noted, however, that the Passage in Genesis 1 states the Divine *Purpose* and the Passage in Genesis 2 states the Divine *Act* of the *same account of Creation.* Genesis 1 tells *what* God did, and Genesis 2 tells briefly *how* God did it. Since the details of the Creation of man are given in Genesis 2, we shall discuss this in the next chapter, which deals with the Dispensation of Innocence.

DAY VII — GOD'S DAY OF REST

So the Bible reveals that God restored the Earth to a second habitable state in six literal 24-hour days of re-creation, and rested on the seventh day. We marvel at the creative Power of our great God! He spoke . . . and it became! *God will not suffer defeat in His program!* What Lucifer destroyed, God restored!

For Further Study

James Montgomery Boice, *Genesis* (Grand Rapids, MI: Zondervan, 1982).

Arthur C. Custance, *Time and Eternity* (Grand Rapids, MI: Zondervan, 1977).

M. R. DeHaan, M.D., *Genesis and Evolution* (Grand Rapids, MI: Zondervan, 1965).

John G. Hall, *God's Dispensational and Prophetic Plan* (Newcastle, OK: John G. Hall, 1985).

Reuben Luther Katter, *The History of Creation and Origin of the Species* (Minneapolis, MN: Theotes Logos Research, Inc., 1967).

Clarence Larkin, *Rightly Dividing the Word* (Glenside, PA: Larkin Estate, 1920).

G. H. Pember, *Earth's Earliest Ages* (Grand Rapids, MI: Kregel, 1975).

Arthur W. Pink, *Gleanings in Genesis* (Chicago, IL: Moody, 1950).

Edward Pusey, *Daniel the Prophet* (Funk and Wagnalls, 1885).

Francis A. Schaeffer, *Genesis in Space and Time* (Downers Grove, IL: Inter Varsity, 1972).

C. I. Scofield, *The Scofield Reference Bible* (New York, NY: Oxford, 1909).

Henry C. Thiessen, *Lectures in Systematic Theology* (Grand Rapids, MI: Eerdmans, 1979).

God's Plan For The Ages

PART
TWO

THE SEVEN DISPENSATIONS

Chapter 5

The Dispensation Of Innocence

CHAPTER FIVE

THE DISPENSATION OF INNOCENCE

DEFINITION OF DISPENSATIONALISM

Dispensationalism is not a new hermeneutical device, for various theologians throughout Church history have had some method of categorizing the dealings of God with man. Augustine wrote, *"Distinguish the ages, and the Scriptures will be in harmony."* A proper understanding of the various Dispensations is essential to *"rightly dividing the Word of Truth"* (II Tim. 2:15).

CREATION OF MAN

The study of the first Dispensation begins with the account of the Creation of man. Genesis 1:26 states that God created man in His Own Image after His Likeness, as previously discussed. Genesis 2:7 gives the detailed account of how God accomplished this:

"And the LORD God formed man of the dust of the ground, and breathed into his nostrils the breath of life; and man became a living soul" (Gen. 2:7).

The Hebrew word translated *"formed"* is *yatsar*, which has reference to a potter molding a piece of clay. The Hebrew word for *"ground"* is *adamah*, which literally means *"red earth,"* from which Adam derived his name. God actually formed the body of man from the dust. *"Out of the ground the LORD God* (also) *formed every beast of the field, and every fowl of the air"* (Gen. 2:19), but the unique feature that distinguished the Creation of man from that of the animals was the infusion of the Spirit from God. When Adam breathed his first breath from the mouth of the Almighty, he *became* a living being. Again, this is a picture of the Triune God in operation. Man is a triunity of body, soul, and spirit. Man *has* a body, he *acquires* a soul, but he *is* a spirit, even as *"God is a Spirit"* (Jn. 4:24). God first molded a lifeless body out of the ground, and then breathed into it *"the breath of lives"* (the Hebrew is plural). This breath of life became the spirit of man, which gave him life:

"The body without the spirit is dead" (James 2:26).

"It is the Spirit Who quickens (gives life)*"* (Jn. 6:63).

When God placed the *spirit* within the *body*, the result produced a third part, and man became a living *soul*. This may explain the plural *"breath of lives."* The inbreathing of God became the *spirit*, and simultaneously, but its action upon the *body*, produced the *soul*. Therefore, man is a tri-chotomous being — body, soul, and spirit:

"For the Word of God is quick (alive), *and powerful, and sharper than any two-edged sword, piercing even to the dividing asunder of soul and spirit, and of the joints and marrow"* (Heb. 4:12).

"And the very God of Peace Sanctify you wholly; and I pray God your whole spirit and soul and body be preserved blameless unto the coming of our Lord Jesus Christ" (I Thess. 5:23).

DISTINCTION BETWEEN BODY, SOUL, AND SPIRIT

The differences between the body, soul, and spirit are various. The *body* is the part of man that houses the soul and spirit. It executes the desires of the soul and spirit (Rom. 7:23-24). The body is the area of human weakness (Mat. 26:41). The Christian's *"body is the Temple of the Holy Spirit"* (I Cor. 6:19), and he will give account at the Judgment Seat of Christ for the deeds done in the body (II Cor. 5:10). The body gives man world-consciousness.

The *soul* is the part of man that *feels*; i.e., the emotions, appetites, and desires:

"And you shall bestow that money for whatsoever YOUR SOUL LUSTS AFTER . . . or for whatsoever YOUR SOUL DESIRES" (Deut. 14:26).

"And she was in BITTERNESS OF SOUL, and prayed unto the Lord, and wept sore" (I Sam 1:10).

"He awakes, and, behold, he is faint, and HIS SOUL HAS APPE-TITE" (Isa. 29:8).

"I will greatly rejoice in the Lord, MY SOUL SHALL BE JOYFUL in My God" (Isa. 61:10).

"And said unto them, MY SOUL IS EXCEEDING SORROWFUL unto death" (Mk. 14:34).

The Greek word translated *"soul"* is *psuche* from which we derive the English word *"psychology,"* the study of human emotions and be-havior. The soul is the battleground of the flesh and spirit (Rom. 8:1-13; I Pet. 2:11; Gal. 5:16-26). The soul gives man self-consciousness.

The *spirit* is the part of man that *knows*; i.e., the mind, will, and intel-lect, which are God given:

"But there is a SPIRIT IN MAN: and the inspiration of the Al-mighty gives them UNDERSTANDING" (Job 32:8).

"Forasmuch as an EXCELLENT SPIRIT, and KNOWLEDGE, and UNDERSTANDING, interpreting of dreams, and showing of hard sentences, and dissolving of doubts, were found in the same Daniel" (Dan. 5:12).

"The SPIRIT indeed is WILLING, but the flesh is weak" (Mat. 26:41).

"For what man KNOWS the things of a man, save THE SPIRIT OF MAN which is in him?" (I Cor. 2:11).

The spirit is formed by God (Zech. 12:1), and is given and taken away by God (Eccl. 12:7; Job 34:14-15). When the appointed time comes, man cannot retain it (Eccl. 8:8). Once the spirit has left the body, the body is dead (James 2:26; Job 27:3, 34:14-15). A resurrection occurs when the spirit again is joined with the body (Lk. 8:53-55). The flesh lusts against the spirit (Gal. 5:17). Christians are to glorify God in spirit and in body (I Cor. 6:20; II Cor. 7:1). The spirit and the soul make up *"the inner man"* (Rom. 7:22; II Cor. 4:16; Eph. 3:16; I Pet. 3:4). The spirit gives man God-consciousness, for it came directly from God, and is the only means by which he is able to apprehend and worship Him.

Although man is a threefold being — body, soul, and spirit — all three separate parts interact as one. For example, in the conversion experience, a person hears the preaching of the Gospel, and the Holy Spirit convicts him of his sins. He senses this conviction in his *soul*, makes a conscious decision to accept Christ in his *spirit*, and goes to the Altar in his *body*. A man can experience the *"joy of sins forgiven"* in his soul *and* his spirit, as Mary the mother of Jesus exclaimed:

"My SOUL doth magnify the Lord, And my SPIRIT has rejoiced in God my Saviour" (Lk. 1:46-47).

Although Salvation usually *is* an emotional experience, it is not *primarily* so, for a person is Born-Again not by *feeling* Saved, but by making an *intelligent decision* to serve the Lord Jesus Christ all the days of his life. It is this ability that distinguishes man from animal, for the enablement to choose Christ as Saviour is possible only as the Holy Spirit deals with man's spirit through the Grace of God.

Therefore, the spirit of man, his intellect, can be a great asset or a grave liability depending on the one he decides to serve — God or Satan. This is the reason why a sinner, who has an unregenerate spirit, can call evil good, and good evil (Isa. 5:20). This is the reason why a Christian must take great care to . . . *"Be not conformed to this world: but be you transformed BY THE RENEWING OF YOUR MIND, that you may prove what is that good, and acceptable, and perfect, Will of God"* (Rom. 12:2).

The Devil constantly is waging battle against the mind of the Christian, and for this reason it is essential that the Believer always wear *"the Helmet of Salvation"* (Eph. 6:17) to win the victory over his attacks.

SUPERIOR INTELLIGENCE OF MAN

Adam was created with an intelligence far superior to that of fallen

49

man, for it is recorded:

"And out of the ground the LORD God formed every beast of the field, and every fowl of the air; and brought them unto Adam to see what he would call them: AND WHATSOEVER ADAM CALLED EVERY LIVING CREATURE, THAT WAS THE NAME THEREOF" (Gen. 2:19).

It was in this perfected state that God took Adam and *"put him into the Garden of Eden to dress it and to keep it"* (Gen. 2:15). After Adam surveyed all of the animal kingdom and inspected the beautiful Garden of God, it became evident to him that *"there was not found a help meet for him"* (Gen. 2:20).

CREATION OF WOMAN

"And the LORD God said, It is not good that the man should be alone; I will make him a help meet for him. And the LORD God caused a deep sleep to fall upon Adam, and he slept: and He took one of his ribs, and closed up the flesh instead thereof; And the rib, which the LORD God had taken from man, made He a woman, and brought her unto the man. And Adam said, This is now bone of my bones, and flesh of my flesh: she shall be called Woman, because she was taken out of Man" (Gen. 2:18, 21-23).

Thus, the man and the woman were both created on the sixth day of Creation, Adam being in existence only a few hours before God formed his wife. Their perfection and innocency are described by the fact that they were both naked and were not ashamed (Gen. 2:25). No doubt, they were clothed with the Shekinah Glory of God.

DEFINITION OF DISPENSATION OF INNOCENCE

The Dispensation of Innocence is also named due to the fact that this was a period of time when man was responsible to God in total sinlessness, innocence, and freedom from guilt. The length of this Dispensation, although not expressly stated, could not have been more than six days for the following reasons.

LENGTH OF THIS DISPENSATION

1. Only one Sabbath day's rest is recorded (Gen. 2:2).
2. Satan, undoubtedly, would have been swift to bring temptation before man.
3. Adam and Eve had not as yet consummated their relationship (Gen. 4:1).

4.   There had not been sufficient enough time for either of them to visit the Tree of Life (Gen. 3:24).

Adam and Eve not only were created supremely intelligent, but also were created with free moral agency — the ability to choose right from wrong. They were not mere puppets controlled by God; they were given the capacity to think and to reason for themselves. This was also true of the Angels and the inhabitants of the original perfect Earth (Isa. 14:12-14; Ezek. 28:14-17). Man was a replica of God in soul and spirit faculties and had a physical body made in the Image and Likeness of God. The Lord placed in the spirit of man the principle and power of obedience, and made a Covenant with him contingent on man's obedience.

EDENIC COVENANT

The Edenic Covenant was given by God to govern the life of man in his unfallen state. The terms were simple:
1.   To be fruitful and multiply and replenish the Earth (Gen. 1:28).
2.   To subdue the Earth and have dominion over the animal kingdom (Gen. 1:28).
3.   To be vegetarian, eating only herbs and fruit (Gen. 1:29).
4.   To dress and keep the Garden of Eden (Gen. 2:15).
5.   To abstain from eating of the Tree of the Knowledge of Good and Evil, under the penalty of death (Gen. 2:17).

COMMAND TO REPLENISH THE EARTH

The command to *"replenish"* the Earth does not necessarily mean to populate the Earth a second time, as discussed in Chapter Two, for the Hebrew word is *mala*, which simply means *"to fill."* It is interesting to note, however, that the translators chose this word, and also used it in Genesis 9:1 where God commanded Noah to *"be fruitful, and multiply, and replenish the Earth."*

Could it have been that the translators of the Authorized Version of the Bible had an understanding of the pre-Adamic Earth and, therefore, chose the word *"replenish"* as the translation of *mala* rather than simply *"to fill"*? It seems only logical that the specific word used in reference to Noah's repopulating the Earth would carry the same connotation in reference to Adam and Eve.

DOMINION OF MAN OVER ALL

The command to subdue the Earth and have dominion over it placed

Adam as the ruler of the Earth, even as Lucifer had been previously (Ezek. 28:14-17). This dominion is described by the Psalmist:

"When I consider Your heavens, the work of Your Fingers, and moon and the stars, which You have ordained; What is man, that You are mindful of him? and the son of man, that You visit him? For You have made him a little lower than the Angels, and have crowned him with glory and honour. YOU MADE HIM TO HAVE DOMINION OVER THE WORKS OF YOUR HANDS; YOU HAVE PUT ALL THINGS UNDER HIS FEET: ALL SHEEP AND OXEN, YEA, AND THE BEASTS OF THE FIELD; THE FOWL OF THE AIR, AND THE FISH OF THE SEA, AND WHATSOEVER PASSES THROUGH THE PATHS OF THE SEAS" (Ps. 8:3-8).

Adam was fully capable of ruling for God in his perfected state, and could have lived forever and never have died!

That God originally planned for man and animals to have a vegetarian diet is stated in Genesis 1:29-30. This also will be the case during the Millennium and the New heavens and the New Earth (Isa. 11:6-9; 65:25). Modern nutritionists have proved that man is much healthier on a high fiber diet including fruits and grains.

The command to dress and keep the Garden proves that man was not idle or lazy while in the Garden of Eden. His work was, no doubt, easier than modern-day agricultural techniques, for there was no thorn, thistle, weed, or blight with which to contend. This surely was the farmer's dream!

TEST OF THIS DISPENSATION

The one particular test that God placed before man during the Dispensation of Innocence was the command that he should not eat of the Tree of the Knowledge of Good and Evil. God's purpose in testing man was to determine whether or not he would be obedient before God and could be trusted to carry out the responsibilities of rulership. Lucifer was anxious to see that man would fail this test, so that once again he could gain dominion over the Earth he once enjoyed.

SERPENT

The instrument Satan used as his mouthpiece to bring temptation before Eve was the serpent. The animal, in this case, should not be confused with a common snake, for this serpent did not become such until after the Fall. We are given several statements that describe him as probably a beautiful being:

   1. He was a beast of the field, but was more subtle, cunning, and

crafty than the others (Gen. 3:1).

2. He could talk and carry on intelligent conversation (Gen. 3:1-6).

3. Eve was not frightened by his presence, but was amazed at his reasoning abilities and was actually deceived by his words (Gen. 3:1-6).

4. He evidently walked upright (Gen. 3:14).

5. He was close to Adam and Eve, and had knowledge of God's Plan for them (Gen. 3:1-15).

The modern concept of Satan as a red devil with horns and a pitchfork is obviously not true. Satan will use whatever tactics are available to him to lure an unsuspecting soul into his trap. If necessary, he can transform himself into *"an angel of light"* (II Cor. 11:14). Such was the case with Eve, for he chose that which would attract her the most effectively. If Eve had avoided the tree altogether, it would have been impossible for her to have eaten of the forbidden fruit. This is the reason why it is so vitally important to *"abstain from all appearance of evil"* (I Thess. 5:22).

TEMPTATION OF MAN

The serpent began his conversation with the woman by *doubting* God's Word — *"Has God said . . . ?"* (Gen. 3:1). He proceeded with *contradicting* God's Word — *"You shall not surely die"* (Gen. 3:4).

Satan has used this same lie down through the centuries, even in the teaching of some churches, that a person can continue in sin and retain his Eternal Life! The serpent then tempted Eve with the very desire that brought about the fall of Lucifer — *"You shall be as gods"* (Gen. 3:5; Isa. 14:14). Insubordination and slander against authority are two sins in which Satan takes great delight in seeing others involved in.

Following this temptation, notice the progression with which Eve succumbed:

"And when the woman SAW that the tree was good for food, and that it was pleasant to the eyes, and a tree to be desired to make one wise, SHE TOOK of the fruit thereof, and DID EAT, and GAVE ALSO UNTO HER HUSBAND with her; and HE DID EAT" (Gen. 3:6).

The first temptation of man had to do with food — the forbidden fruit — and the first temptation of Jesus had to do with food — turning stones into bread (Lk. 4:3). Satan tempts man easiest in the area of his appetites, and he tempted Eve with all three categories of temptation the world has to offer:

1. The lust of the flesh;

2. The lust of the eyes; and,

3. The pride of life (I Jn. 2:16).

Eve *saw* the tree, she *took* of the fruit, and *did eat.* As is usually the case — others are affected by their own sin — she gave to Adam and *"he did eat"* (Gen. 3:6). This is the natural progression of temptation leading to sin:

"Let no man say when he is tempted, I am tempted of God: for God cannot be tempted with evil, neither tempts He any man: But every man is TEMPTED, WHEN HE IS DRAWN AWAY OF HIS OWN LUST, AND ENTICED. Then when LUST has CONCEIVED, it BRINGS FORTH SIN: and SIN, WHEN IT IS FINISHED, BRINGS FORTH DEATH" (James 1:13-15).

FALL OF MAN

When Adam and Eve ate of the fruit, they immediately lost their innocence and sinless countenance and knew that they were naked. They also lost:

1. Spiritual, physical, and Eternal Life as God had promised (Gen. 2:17);
2. Fellowship with God and the Creation (Gen. 3:15);
3. Dominion over the Earth (Ps. 8:3-8);
4. The Perfect Image of God (Gen. 1:27);
5. The right to the Tree of Life (Gen. 3:22-24);
6. Their home in the Garden of Eden (Gen. 3:22-24); and,
7. Freedom from disease, sorrow, afflictions, and suffering (Gen. 3:16-19).

The man and his wife were ASHAMED and sought to cover their nakedness with aprons made out of fig leaves (Gen. 3:7). The fact that they were ashamed was the one ray of hope for their future. For if they had lost their ability to sense the shame of guilt, they would have been no different than evil spirits, and their Salvation would have been impossible. Although the God-consciousness within their spirit had been overwhelmed, it had not been totally extinguished.

After this, Adam and Eve heard the Voice of God as He walked in the Garden. The Voice that once had been their greatest joy now became their greatest fear, and they fled trying to hide from the all-seeing, all-knowing, all-mighty God.

God first of all called unto the man, Adam, who answered the Lord, saying that he had heard His Voice, but was afraid because he was naked. When God asked Adam if he had eaten of the Tree of the Knowledge of Good and Evil, he passed the blame to his wife, Eve:

"The woman whom You gave to be with me, SHE GAVE ME OF THE TREE, and I did eat" (Gen. 3:12).

Actually, Adam partially was blaming God as well, saying, in essence, *"If You hadn't given me this woman, I wouldn't have eaten of the tree!"*

God then inquired of Eve, who passed the blame on to the serpent:

"The SERPENT BEGUILED ME, and I did eat" (Gen. 3:13).

CURSE UPON SERPENT, WOMAN, MAN, AND EARTH

After God patiently gave the couple the opportunity to defend their actions, He turned to the serpent and His Attitude changed dramatically. God did not give Satan the opportunity to defend himself, but treated him as already condemned. The words that God spoke to the serpent partially are fulfilled in the serpent and partially fulfilled in Satan, for the law of double reference, as discussed in Chapter Two, is applied. The words spoken to the serpent also mark the beginning of the second great covenant in Scripture — the Adamic Covenant:

"And the Lord God said unto the SERPENT, Because you have done this, you are CURSED above all cattle, and above every beast of the field; upon your belly shall you go, and dust shall you eat all the days of your life: And I will put enmity between you and the woman, and between your seed and her Seed; it shall bruise your head, and you shall bruise His Heel" (Gen. 3:14-15).

The curse upon the serpent will continue even throughout the Millennium, when the curse will be lifted from the other animals. This will be a constant reminder of the wages of sin to the inhabitants of the Earth (Isa. 65:25). Satan clearly is referred to by the phrase *"I will put enmity between you and the woman, and between your seed and her Seed,"* for the woman knew clearly that her false friend was the cause of all her misery. From this day forth she would regard him as her worst enemy!

The *"seed"* of the serpent refers to natural snakes, the descendants of the original serpent, but also has a double reference to all ungodly men, who are called children of the Devil (Jn. 8:44). The *"seed"* of the woman refers to the natural descendants of Eve, and to one *"Seed"* in particular, the Lord Jesus Christ! Genesis 3:15 is the first Prophecy concerning the Redeemer defeating Satan at Calvary!

Following the curse of the serpent (which included Satan), God turned His attention to the woman:

"Unto the woman he said, I will greatly multiply your sorrow and your conception; in sorrow you shall bring forth children; and your desire shall be to your husband, and he shall rule over you" (Gen. 3:16).

The curse upon the woman included a painful process of childbirth, and the forfeiture of her co-equal status with her husband — *"He shall rule over you"* (Gen. 3:16).

God next addressed Adam:

"And unto Adam He said, Because You have hearkened unto the

voice of your wife, and have eaten of the tree, of which I commanded you, saying, You shall not eat of it: CURSED is the ground for your sake; in sorrow shall you eat of it all the days of your life; Thorns also and thistles shall it bring forth to you; and you shall eat the herb of the field; In the sweat of your face shall you eat bread, till you return unto the ground; for out of it were you taken: for dust you are, and unto dust shall you return" (Gen. 3:17-19).

Because Adam had been given dominion over all the Earth, and was commanded to care for the Garden, the curse upon man extended beyond himself, to the very ground from which he was formed. In the final analysis DEATH was the ultimate curse upon the entire Creation. What God had spoken, He was faithful to perform: *"In the day that you eat thereof you shall surely die"* (Gen. 2:17).

PROMISE OF A REDEEMER

Although God was bound to punish sin, He did not forsake the man and the woman who He cared for with an everlasting love. God made a covering for Adam and Eve from the skins of animals He slew as an example of the sacrifices they should offer in looking forward to the promised Redeemer!

And so, the Dispensation of Innocence ended with this expression of God's Love.

Chapter 6

The Dispensation Of Conscience

CHAPTER SIX

THE DISPENSATION OF CONSCIENCE

EXPULSION FROM THE GARDEN

The Dispensation of Conscience began with man *outside* of the paradise God has made especially for him. The Lord placed Cherubim at the east of Eden to guard the Tree of Life, for if Adam and Eve had eaten of that tree, they would have lived forever in their fallen state (Gen. 3:22-24). It is stated that *"the saddest thought of tongue or pen is wondering what might have been,"* and this certainly must have been the sentiment of the first man and woman.

BEGINNING OF SACRIFICIAL OFFERINGS

The only hope God had given was the Promise of the *"Seed"* of the woman bruising the head of the serpent (Gen. 3:15). Although they could not have understood the full ramifications of this Promise, they offered sacrifices unto the Lord that typified the fulfillment of this Prophecy. They also taught their children to honor God with their substance (Gen. 4:4-5).

DEFINITION OF DISPENSATION OF CONSCIENCE

The Dispensation of Conscience is given this designation due to the fact that man during this period was tested on the basis of obedience to his own conscience. The dictionary defines *"conscience"* as *"the sense or consciousness of the moral goodness or blameworthiness of one's own conduct, intentions, or character together with a feeling or obligation to do right or be good."* The Apostle Paul described this Dispensation in his Epistle to the Romans:

"For when the Gentiles, which have not the Law, do by nature the things contained in the Law, these, having not the Law, are a Law unto themselves: Which show the work of the Law written in their hearts, their CONSCIENCE ALSO BEARING WITNESS, AND THEIR THOUGHTS THE MEAN WHILE ACCUSING OR ELSE EXCUSING ONE ANOTHER" (Rom. 2:14-15).

The title for this Dispensation does not imply that man was without a conscience before or after this period, anymore than the Dispensation of the Law suggests that there was not Law before or after this period. It simply suggests that God governed mankind during this economy through his conscience, in a predominant manner. Obedience to the dictates of the conscience was man's chief stewardship responsibility and accountability to God. *"Let your conscience be your guide"* proved to be a poor code of ethics.

LENGTH OF THIS DISPENSATION

The Dispensation of Conscience lasted 1,656 years — from the expulsion from the Garden of Eden to the Flood of Noah. By studying the genealogy of Genesis 5:1-29; 7:11 this span of time is easily calculated:

     130   years from Adam to the birth of Seth
     105   years from Seth to the birth of Enos
      90   years from Enos to the birth of Cainan
      70   years from Cainan to the birth of Mahalaleel
      65   years from Mahalaleel to the birth of Jared
     162   years from Jared to the birth of Enoch
      65   years from Enoch to the birth of Methuselah
     187   years from Methuselah to the birth of Lamech
     182   years from Lamech to the birth of Noah
     <u>600</u>   years from Noah to the Flood
 1,656   years from the expulsion from the Garden of Eden to the Flood of Noah

TEST OF THIS DISPENSATION

God's Purpose in the Dispensation of Conscience was to see if man would voluntarily serve Him or Satan. Without coercion or restraint, God gave man the opportunity to choose who his master would be.

This was actually an *"age of freedom,"* for man was free to be led by his conscience or to disobey his conscience, without fear of being apprehended by the Law. Through this Dispensation, man would learn how sinful he could become by choosing to live selfishly without regard for others.

SACRIFICES OF CAIN AND ABEL

Such was the case with the firstborn sons of Adam and Eve. Cain and Abel were taught the importance of offering sacrifice unto the Lord. Cain, being a farmer, brought his produce to offer on the Altar. Abel, who had become a shepherd, brought the firstlings of his flock to offer before the Lord. God accepted the offering of Abel, but rejected Cain's, for *"without shedding of blood is no remission* (of sin)" (Heb. 9:22).

MURDER OF ABEL AND PUNISHMENT OF CAIN

Even though God gave Cain another chance, and explained to him the importance of the Sin Offering (Gen. 4:6-7), Cain was overcome with jealousy and murdered his brother. Because of this great sin, Cain was to become a fugitive and a vagabond, but the Lord placed a protective mark upon Cain, which was an oath that whoever killed him would receive judgment sevenfold.

CITY OF CAIN

Cain and his wife dwelt in the land of Nod, where their son was born. Cain built a city and named it after his son, Enoch.

The question is often asked, *"Where did Cain get his wife?"* Obviously, he took one of Adam's daughters (Gen. 5:4) to be his wife. Such a marriage could not have been avoided since the entire human race descended from a single pair! After the world had been populated adequately, this was strongly forbidden.

Some persons also have wondered where Cain found enough people to build a city. Understanding that the average life span was 800 or 900 years, a person easily can see how quickly the human race could have multiplied. Also, many years after Cain's flight from Eden may have passed before he built the city.

LIFE-STYLE OF THIS DISPENSATION

Cain's descendants and their occupations give insight into the lifestyle of the Dispensation of Conscience. We know nothing of the generations following Enoch until we come to Lamech who was the fifth from Cain. Lamech broke the primeval law of marriage and became the first polygamist, which shows the ongoing deterioration of the family of the Cainites. Lamech also committed murder, apparently killing someone who had caused him harm (Gen. 4:23).

The sons of Lamech were (1) *Jabal*, who was the first to dwell in tents and was also the first rancher, making a living raising cattle; (2) *Jubal*, who invented the harp and the organ to be used in song and dance; and, (3) *Tubal-cain*, who invented the mechanical arts and designed weapons of brass and iron. Jabal's ranching abilities probably introduced flesh and milk as food, to escape tilling the soil. Jubal's music added to the pleasures of a crowded society. Tubal-cain's brass and iron instruments were used as weapons of war in a violent land (Gen. 6:13).

This is the last record of the family tree of Cain as separated from the rest of the world. Its first ancestor was a murderer — Cain; its last recorded descendant was a polygamist *and* a murderer — Lamech. Sin not only had increased, but had begun to fill the entire Earth (Gen. 6:11).

DESCENDANTS OF SETH

Adam and Eve had another son and called his name Seth, which means *"substituted,"* in view of Abel's death. Some Bible scholars have sought to prove that although the lineage of Cain was wicked, Seth's lineage was Godly. However, this is only partly true, for only Enoch and Noah are mentioned as being righteous. There is no basis in Scripture to conclude that the other descendants of Seth were any different than the descendants of Cain as far as righteousness is concerned. Enoch, the seventh from Adam (not to be confused with Cain's first son), was not only a Godly and righteous man, but a Prophet as well:

"And Enoch also, the seventh from Adam, Prophesied of these, saying, Behold, the Lord comes with ten thousands of His Saints, To execute Judgment upon all, and to convince all who are ungodly among them of all their ungodly deeds which they have ungodly committed, and of all their hard speeches which ungodly sinners have spoken against Him" (Jude, Vss. 14-15).

TRANSLATION OF ENOCH

As the Earth continued in sin and rebellion against God, there was a prophetic voice being heard! Not only did Enoch warn of the coming Judgment of God upon unrighteousness, but he also proclaimed the Message of the Second Coming of Christ! It is no secret why the record reveals that *"Enoch walked with God: and he was not; for God took him"* (Gen. 5:23-24). God *"raptured"* Enoch from the Earth before the coming Judgment of Noah's Flood, even as God will translate all of the Believers who walk with God now, before the coming Tribulation!

Enoch's son Methuselah is best known as the oldest man who ever lived, for he died at the age of 969. Actually, his father Enoch is *truly* the oldest man who ever lived, for he lived 365 years on the Earth, and has lived for over 5,000 years in Heaven in his natural flesh-and-blood body! Enoch will come back during the Tribulation days, as one of the two witnesses of Revelation, Chapter 11, and will be killed by his enemies, but will be resurrected three and one-half days later with a glorified body and taken to Heaven (Rev. 11:3-12).

The *name* of Methuselah was also a testimony to the wicked generation that Judgment was approaching. His name signifies, *"WHEN HE IS DEAD, IT SHALL BE SENT"*; i.e., the Deluge or Flood. This name strongly implies that God had given Enoch a Revelation of the coming Judgment of God when he named his son. God said that the Flood was to come after the death of that son. This explains the Verse:

"And Enoch walked with God AFTER HE BEGAT Methuselah three hundred years, and begat sons and daughters" (Gen. 5:22).

This also explains the fact why Methuselah lived so much longer than the average man — God's Grace was being extended to a wicked and rebellious people. While Methuselah *lived*, the Flood would be held back. But when he *died*, it would come! And it did, IN THE VERY YEAR!

The last mention we have of Adam before the Flood is given in Genesis, Chapter 6:

"And the Lord said, My Spirit shall not always strive with man (Hebrew, *adamah*, literally *"the man"*), *for that he also is flesh: yet his days shall be an hundred and twenty years"* (Gen. 6:3).

God gave Adam 120 additional years in which to repent of his failure. Whether or not he *did* repent is not revealed.

SONS OF GOD AND DAUGHTERS OF MEN

The ultimate sin that ushered in the swift wrath of God destroying all mankind is revealed in Genesis, Chapter 6:

"And it came to pass, when men began to multiply on the face of the Earth, and daughters were born unto them, That the SONS OF GOD saw the DAUGHTERS OF MEN that they were fair; AND THEY TOOK THEM WIVES OF ALL WHICH THEY CHOSE. There were GIANTS in the Earth IN THOSE DAYS; and ALSO AFTER THAT, when the SONS OF GOD CAME IN UNTO THE DAUGHTERS OF MEN, AND THEY BORE CHILDREN TO THEM, the same became mighty men which were of old, men of renown" (Gen. 6:1-2, 4).

Everyone agrees that the *"daughters of men"* refers to the human women who lived on the Earth prior to the Flood. There is, however, much controversy as to who the *"sons of God"* that cohabited with the women of the Earth actually were. There are basically two opinions.

Some interpreters say that the *"sons of God"* were the descendants of the so-called Godly line of Seth, who according to this interpretation would be said to have married unbelieving women.

The other opinion, which, it seems, has more Scriptural and historical support, states that *"sons of God"* refers to Angels. There is only one argument generally given opposing this latter view, and that is the statement of Jesus:

"The children of this world marry, and are given in marriage: But they which shall be accounted worthy to obtain that world, and the Resurrection from the dead, neither marry, nor are given in marriage: neither can they die any more: for THEY ARE EQUAL UNTO THE ANGELS; and are the Children of God, being the Children of the Resurrection" (Lk. 20:34-36).

However, a proper understanding of this Passage only reveals that the Angels never marry among themselves, for they have no need of perpetuating a race. Also, this Scripture is futuristic in application — *"of the Resurrection"* — and would not have reference to the period of time stated in Genesis, Chapter 6. Besides, this one objection is hardly plausible when all evidence supporting this view is clearly understood:

IDENTITY OF SONS OF GOD

1. The terms *"sons of God"* and *"daughters of men"* clearly indicate two separate classes of created beings or personalities. If *"sons of God"* is supposed to refer to the Godly line of Seth, why was the phrase *"sons of Adam," "sons of Seth,"* or even *"SONS OF MEN"* not used?

2. Of the three times the term *"sons of God"* is used in the Old Testament, other than Genesis, Chapter 6, it is used to describe Angels EVERY TIME:

"Now there was a day when the SONS OF GOD came to present themselves before the LORD, and Satan came also among them" (Job 1:6).

"Again there was a day when the SONS OF GOD came to present themselves before the LORD, and Satan came also among them to present himself before the LORD" (Job 2:1).

"Where were you when I laid the foundations of the Earth? . . . When the morning stars sang together, and all the SONS OF GOD shouted for joy?" (Job 38:4-7).

3. The Septuagint, which is the Greek version of the Old Testament, translated in 285 B.C., and used by Christ and the Apostles, reads, *"the ANGELS OF GOD . . . took them wives of all they chose"* (Gen. 6:2).

4. The Book of Jude refers to this sin of the fallen Angels:

"And the Angels which kept not THEIR FIRST ESTATE, but LEFT THEIR OWN HABITATION, He has reserved in everlasting chains under darkness unto the Judgment of the Great Day. Even as Sodom and Gomorrah, and the cities about them IN LIKE MANNER, GIVING THEMSELVES OVER TO FORNICATION, AND

GOING AFTER STRANGE FLESH, are set forth for an example, suffering the vengeance of eternal fire" (Jude, Vss. 6-7).

This Passage clearly states that a certain class of Angels left their own proper place and are specifically under Judgment because they acted like the people of Sodom and Gomorrah. As the Sodomites sought *"other flesh"* (as the Greek reads) in the sin of homosexuality, these Angels sought after *"other flesh,"* by involving themselves with human women in the sin of fornication.

5.   The Apostle Peter stated that this sin occurred during the time of Noah:

"For if God spared not THE ANGELS WHO SINNED, but cast them down to Hell, and delivered them into chains of darkness, to be reserved unto Judgment; AND SPARED NOT THE OLD WORLD, BUT SAVED NOAH the eighth person, a Preacher of Righteousness, BRINGING IN THE FLOOD UPON THE WORLD OF THE UNGODLY" (II Pet. 2:4-5).

Peter also stated how God judged these fallen Angels for their great sin.

6.   The Apostle Peter stated that after Jesus died on the Cross, He went and preached to these fallen Angels:

"By which also HE WENT AND PREACHED UNTO THE SPIRITS IN PRISON; WHICH SOMETIME WERE DISOBEDIENT, WHEN ONCE THE LONGSUFFERING OF GOD WAITED IN THE DAYS OF NOAH, WHILE THE ARK WAS A PREPARING, wherein few, that is, eight souls were saved by water" (I Pet. 3:19-20).

The Scriptures could not state it more plainly, that these *"sons of God"* were indeed Angels who committed fornication with women.

7.   The ancient Jewish Book of I Enoch, which is quoted from in Jude, Verses 14 and 15 (I Enoch 1:9), referring to Enoch, also gives greater detail concerning the *"sons of God"* being Angels:

"And it came to pass when the children of men had multiplied that in those days were born unto them beautiful and comely daughters, AND THE ANGELS, THE CHILDREN OF HEAVEN, SAW AND LUSTED AFTER THEM, AND SAID TO ONE ANOTHER: 'COME LET US CHOOSE US WIVES FROM AMONG THE CHILDREN OF MEN AND BEGET US CHILDREN' . . . They were in all two hundred . . . THEY TOOK UNTO THEMSELVES WIVES, AND EACH CHOSE FOR HIMSELF ONE, AND THEY BEGAN TO GO IN UNTO THEM AND TO DEFILE THEMSELVES WITH THEM, and they taught them charms and enchantments . . . AND THEY BECAME PREGNANT, AND THEY BARE GREAT GIANTS, WHOSE HEIGHT WAS THREE THOUSAND ELLS . . . And there arose much godlessness, and they

committed fornication, and they were led astray, and became corrupt in all their ways" (I Enoch 6-8).

Although I Enoch is not a Biblical Book, and is not Divinely inspired, the fact that Jude quoted from it does give the book *historical* credibility. It is also apparent that both Jude, the brother of our Lord, and the Apostle Peter, in their brief references to the same subject, it seems, agreed with it — at least in this matter.

8. This was also the view of many theological giants of Church history, such as Chrysostom, Augustine, Luther, and Calvin.

9. The offspring of *"giants"* (Gen. 6:4) must have required some kind of superhuman sire. The truth of the matter is that this sin of fallen Angels cohabitating with women occurred both before *and* after the Flood (Gen. 6:4). The giants after the Flood occupied the land of Canaan (Num. 13:26-33) and continued to oppress Israel until Kind David saw that the last of the giants were killed (I Sam. 17:4-51; II Sam. 21:15-22; I Chron. 20:4-8).

10. God prepared a special place of punishment for the Angels who fell and committed fornication. It is called *tartaros* in the Greek and is translated *"Hell"* in II Peter 2:4, with reference to these fallen Angels. This is the only time this word is used in the entire Bible, and describes a place of torment in the deepest recesses of Hell, especially for the judgment of this sin.

And so, it has been proved, both Scripturally and historically, that the sin of Angels cohabitating with the *"daughters of men"* stirred the wrath of God to the point that He grieved over having created man to begin with, and planned to destroy every living creature from off the face of the Earth. Satan's desire in bringing about this unnatural and unholy relationship between Angels and women was to corrupt the entire human race, so that Christ, the Seed of the woman, could not come into the world. He ALMOST succeeded, for there was only ONE MAN who, along with his family, remained faithful to God:

"BUT NOAH FOUND GRACE IN THE EYES OF THE LORD!" (Gen. 6:8).

The times of Noah had become sordid beyond any full description. It is ironic that although there was violence, murder, sexual perversion, and all kinds of rebellion against God in the land, there was also luxury, a refined culture, and a love of art and music. Such minglings of otherwise incongruous activities have not been infrequent in past history, such as the times of ancient Rome and Greece. Such is also the case is modern times, in our own land! Jesus prophesied that the days of Noah would be repeated in the Endtimes, culminating in the seven years of Tribulation:

"And as it was in the days of Noah, so shall it be also in the days of

the Son of Man. They did eat, they drank, they married wives, they were given in marriage, until the day that Noah entered into the Ark, and the flood came, and destroyed them all" (Lk. 17:26-27).

If Noah had not remained faithful to God, the Lord would have destroyed the entire human race, even as He did the pre-Adamic world over which Lucifer reigned (Jer. 4:23-26; II Pet. 3:4-7).

NOAH'S ARK

God instructed Noah to build an Ark, and gave him the exact dimensions to follow (Gen. 6:14-16). He also allowed Noah to preach during the entire time he was building the Ark, in hope that some persons would turn from their wicked ways. God also instructed Noah to take two of every species of animal in the Earth, male and female, to perpetuate the animal kingdom. Noah further was commanded to take seven pairs of the clean animals, male and female, into the Ark so that the sacrifice could continue (Gen. 6:17 through 7:3).

FLOOD

When Noah was 600 years old (Gen. 7:6), he took his wife, his three sons, Ham, Shem, and Japheth, and their wives; and they, along with the animals, entered into the Ark of safety. Noah and his family were, no doubt, ridiculed and made fun of for obeying the Voice of the Lord. But when it began to rain, the laughing ceased! Man's fateful day had arrived! The sorrowful thing is that man had been warned time and time again, by Enoch and Noah, but had chosen to go his own way. Man's conscience had led him to death and destruction! What a horrible day it must have been when Noah and his family heard the people outside the Ark, banging on the sides of the boat, screaming in horror as the waters began to rise above the Earth!

The waters rose above the mountaintops, killing every living creature (Gen. 7:17-23). After 40 days, the rain ceased, but the waters remained on the Earth for 150 days (Gen. 7:24). As the waters began to recede, the Ark rested on Mount Ararat (Gen. 8:4). Noah opened the window of the Ark and sent forth a raven, *"which went forth to and fro,"* without finding a place to rest (Gen. 8:7). He then sent forth a dove, which *"found no rest . . . and* (so returned) *unto him into the Ark"* (Gen. 8:8-9). Seven days later, Noah sent the dove out of the Ark again, and the bird returned with an olive leaf, proving that the waters had abated (Gen. 8:10-11). One more week passed and Noah sent forth the dove, which did not return, for the Earth's surface had dried (Gen. 8:12).

PROMISE

After Noah and his family had been in the Ark for one year and 17 days (Gen. 7:10-11; 8:13-14), he opened the door of the Ark, and he and his family entered a new Dispensation of time.

Thus, the Dispensation of Conscience ended with Judgment and death, even as the Dispensation of Innocence had ended. But God also gave man a Promise, symbolized by the rainbow (Gen. 9:13). The same God who hates sin, and will judge it severely, is the same loving Father who cares for His Own.

Chapter 7

The Dispensation Of Human Government

CHAPTER SEVEN

THE DISPENSATION OF HUMAN GOVERNMENT

When Noah and his family stepped out of the Ark, the first thing they did was give thanks unto the Lord. This is the secret of having God's Blessings upon a family. God was pleased with Noah's offering and made a Covenant with him, saying:

"I will not again curse the ground any more for man's sake; for the imagination of man's heart is evil from his youth; neither will I again smite any more every thing living, as I have done. While the Earth remains, seedtime and harvest, and cold and heat, and summer and winter, and day and night shall not cease" (Gen. 8:21-22).

God blessed Noah and his family and gave them the same command He had given to Adam and Eve:

"Be fruitful, and multiply, and REPLENISH the Earth" (Gen. 9:1).

There are other similarities between the First Family and Noah's family. Both were given the responsibility of repopulating the Earth after a major calamity. Both existed at the beginning of a new Dispensation. Both were eyewitnesses of God's Punishment upon sin. Both offered sacrifices to God.

LENGTH OF THIS DISPENSATION

The Dispensation of Human Government is the third Dispensation of man and covers the events after the Flood to the Call of Abraham — a total of 427 years. The length of this period is calculated by studying the genealogy listed in Genesis 11:10-32:

    2 years from the Flood to the birth of Arphaxad
  35 years from Arphaxad to the birth of Salah
  30 years from Salah to the birth of Eber
  34 years from Eber to the birth of Peleg
  30 years from Peleg to the birth of Reu
  32 years from Reu to the birth of Serug
  30 years from Serug to the birth of Nahor
  29 years from Nahor to the birth of Terah
<u>205</u> years later Terah died in Haran
427 years from the Flood to the Call of Abraham

Abraham was 75 years of age when Terah died, and he received his

Call to leave Ur of the Chaldees and to go into the land of Canaan.

DEFINITION OF DISPENSATION
OF HUMAN GOVERNMENT

This Dispensation is called the Dispensation of Human Government due to the fact that God gave Noah and his descendants certain laws with which to govern the human race:
1. To repopulate the Earth (Gen. 9:1, 7);
2. To exercise dominion over the animals (Gen. 9:2);
3. To eat meat as well as fruits and vegetables (Gen. 9:3);
4. Not to eat the flesh of animals containing the blood (Gen. 9:4); and,
5. To institute capital punishment for murder (Gen. 9:5-6).

GOD'S MORAL ABSOLUTES

This was the first time that man was given the authority to govern the affairs of man, under God. The first two laws listed above were also in effect in the Dispensation of Innocence and the Dispensation of Conscience. The addition of animal flesh to the diet, no doubt, was allowed by God due to the scarcity of produce following the Flood. Man, however, was not allowed to eat meat that contained blood. God intended man to respect the sanctity of life.

DIVINE INSTITUTION OF
CAPITAL PUNISHMENT

Capital punishment was now instituted to increase further man's regard for life. Although God did not require death for the sin of murder in the Dispensation of Conscience, due to there being no stated law, He did so in this Dispensation and has in every Dispensation since then. Under the Law, God commanded the death of all murderers (Ex. 21:12). In this Dispensation of Grace, God upholds civil governments and their duty to administer capital punishment to deserving criminals:

"Let every soul be subject unto the higher powers. For there is no power but of God: THE POWERS THAT BE ARE ORDAINED OF GOD. WHOSOEVER THEREFORE RESISTS THE POWER, RESISTS THE ORDINANCE OF GOD: AND THEY WHO RESIST SHALL RECEIVE TO THEMSELVES DAMNATION. For rulers are not a terror to good works, but to the evil. Will you then not be afraid of the power? do that which is good, and you shall have praise of the same: For he is the MINISTER OF GOD to you for good. BUT IF

YOU DO THAT WHICH IS EVIL, BE AFRAID; FOR HE BEARS NOT THE SWORD IN VAIN: FOR HE IS THE MINISTER OF GOD, A REVENGER TO EXECUTE WRATH UPON HIM WHO DOES EVIL" (Rom. 13:1-4).

Capital punishment also will be administered during the Millennial Reign of Jesus Christ (Isa. 11:3-9; 65:20). It is necessary to punish criminals according to the crimes committed, otherwise society would crumble. Although there may be inequities in the present judicial system, there will *not* be when Jesus comes back to Earth again! God has ordained human governments to assist Him in administering justice until He personally returns.

Christians should support the government and their elected officials. Even in the most wicked times of the Roman Empire, the Apostle Peter wrote:

"Submit yourselves to EVERY Ordinance of man for the Lord's sake: whether it be to the KING, as supreme; Or unto GOVERNORS, as unto them who are sent by him FOR THE PUNISHMENT OF EVILDOERS, and for the praise of them who do well. Honour all men. Love the brotherhood. Fear God. HONOUR THE KING" (I Pet. 2:13-14, 17).

The Apostle Paul also admonished Timothy:

"I exhort therefore, that, first of all, supplications, prayers, intercessions, and giving of thanks, be made for all men; FOR KINGS, AND FOR ALL WHO ARE IN AUTHORITY; that we may lead a quiet and peaceable life in all Godliness and honesty" (I Tim. 2:1-2).

Christians have a moral obligation to become involved in the electoral process, to see that Godly officials are elected to administer the laws of the land. Christians also should pray for those who hold public offices.

NOAHIC COVENANT

So, we see that human government was instituted first in the days of Noah, following the Flood. Noah and his family settled in the mountainous area of Ararat called Armenia. This was a fertile land, well suited for habitation. When Noah looked up at the sky, he saw the beautiful rainbow of which God said:

"I DO SET MY BOW IN THE CLOUD, and IT SHALL BE FOR A TOKEN OF A COVENANT BETWEEN ME AND THE EARTH. And it shall come to pass, when I bring a cloud over the Earth, that the bow shall be seen in the cloud: AND I WILL REMEMBER MY COVENANT, which is between Me and you and every living creature of

all flesh; and the waters shall no more become a flood to destroy all flesh. AND THE BOW SHALL BE IN THE CLOUD; and I will look upon it, that I MAY REMEMBER the Everlasting Covenant between God and every living creature of all flesh that is upon the Earth" (Gen. 9:13-16).

God said, *"I WILL REMEMBER"!* This is one of the greatest Promises God has ever made to man. What God has stated in His Word, He is faithful to perform! The writer of Hebrews stated:

"Let us hold fast the profession of our Faith without wavering; (FOR HE IS FAITHFUL WHO PROMISED)" (Heb. 10:23).

The Promises that God made to His People Israel surely will be fulfilled. Although the Israelites are presently in rebellion against the Lord, God once again will deal with Israel as a nation, and they once again will turn to God and accept Jesus Christ as their Messiah. The Apostle Paul taught this:

"For I would not, Brethren, that you should be ignorant of this mystery, lest you should be wise in your own conceits; THAT BLINDNESS IN PART IS HAPPENED TO ISRAEL, UNTIL THE FULNESS OF THE GENTILES BE COME IN. AND SO ALL IS-RAEL SHALL BE SAVED: AS IT IS WRITTEN, THERE SHALL COME OUT OF SION THE DELIVERER, AND SHALL TURN AWAY UNGODLINESS FROM JACOB: FOR THIS IS MY COV-ENANT UNTO THEM, WHEN I SHALL TAKE AWAY THEIR SINS" (Rom. 11:25-27).

In the next chapter we shall discuss the Covenant God made with Israel, but briefly let us note that God is still dealing with Israel because of His Promise:

"Remember these, O Jacob and Israel; for you are My servant: I have formed you; you are My servant: O Israel, YOU SHALL NOT BE FORGOTTEN OF ME" (Isa. 44:21).

God will never forget His Children, and God will not forget to bless His Children when they are in need. Every good work that is done for the Lord will be blessed:

"GOD IS NOT UNRIGHTEOUS TO FORGET YOUR WORK AND LABOUR OF LOVE, WHICH YOU HAVE SHOWED TOWARD HIS NAME, IN THAT YOU HAVE MINISTERED TO THE SAINTS, AND DO MINISTER" (Heb. 6:10).

God keeps His Promises to those who believe Him! This was stated so beautifully by John the Revelator:

"He who sat was to look upon like a jasper and a sardine stone: and THERE WAS A RAINBOW ROUND ABOUT THE THRONE, in sight like unto an emerald" (Rev. 4:3).

The Lord forever is reminded of the glorious Promises He has extended to us, when He beholds the beautiful rainbow around His Throne! That is the reason we are commanded in the Word of God:

"Let us therefore come boldly unto the THRONE OF GRACE, that we may obtain Mercy, and find Grace to help in time of need" (Heb. 4:16).

Not only does the rainbow *in the sky* remind God of the Covenant He made with Noah, but the rainbow *around His Throne* reminds Him of the Promises He has made to each Believer! As the old song so appropriately states:

"God is still on the Throne, and He will remember His Own;
"Though trials may press us and burdens distress us,
"He never will leave us alone; God is still on the Throne,
"He never forsaketh His Own; His Promise is True,
"He will not forget you, God is still on the Throne!"

NOAH, A FARMER

After the Flood, Noah became a farmer and planted a vineyard. This was intended most likely to supplement the lack of good fruits and vegetables available to him and his family after the destruction of the Deluge.

NOAH'S FAILURE

Whether it was intentional, or due to his inexperience with the fruit of the vine, Noah became drunk! While he was in this inebriated condition, Ham, the youngest son of Noah, *"saw the nakedness of his father, and told his two brethren without"* (Gen. 9:22).

Although we are not given all of the details, it appears that Ham made fun of his father in his drunken and humiliating state, and called his brothers, Shem and Japheth, also to come and mock him. Ham's brothers showed much maturity and respect for their father by not mocking him, but by covering him with a garment, so that his nakedness was not seen (Gen. 9:22-23).

SIMILARITIES BETWEEN ADAM AND NOAH

Earlier we discussed the similarities between Adam's family and Noah's family. There are also similarities between Adam and Noah as individuals.

Adam faced an Earth just restored from a flood of Judgment (Gen. 1:2). Noah stepped out of the Ark onto an Earth that had just experienced a great Flood sent as Divine Judgment upon sin (Gen. 8:14).

Adam was given dominion over Creation (Gen. 1:28). God delivered all things into the hands of Noah (Gen. 9:2).

God placed Adam in a Garden and commanded him to dress and keep it (Gen. 2:15). Noah became a husbandman and planted a vineyard (Gen. 9:20).

Eating the fruit of a tree in this Garden caused Adam's fall (Gen. 3:6). Drinking the fruit of the vine in Noah's garden caused his fall (Gen. 9:21).

Adam's sin resulted in the exposure of his nakedness (Gen. 3:7). Noah's sin had the same results (Gen. 9:21). Adam's nakedness was covered (Gen. 3:21), as was Noah's (Gen. 9:23).

This sin of Adam brought a curse upon his descendants (Rom. 5:12). Noah's sin brought a curse upon his posterity (Gen. 9:24-25).

Adam had three sons — Cain, Abel, and Seth; Seth was the son through whom the promised Seed would come (Gen. 4:25; Lk. 3:23-38). Noah had three sons — Japheth, Shem, and Ham; Shem was the son through whom Jesus was descended (Gen. 9:26; Lk. 3:23-36).

CURSE UPON HAM

When Noah awakened out of his drunkenness, he discovered what his son Ham had done to him. He then pronounced a curse upon Ham's descendants and a blessing upon the descendants of Shem and Japheth:

"And he said, Cursed be Canaan (Ham's son); a servant of servants shall he be unto his brethren. And he said, Blessed be the LORD God of Shem; and Canaan shall be his servant. God shall enlarge Japheth, and he shall dwell in the tents of Shem; and Canaan shall be his servant" (Gen. 9:25-27).

SHEM, HAM, AND JAPHETH

Ham's descendants were relegated to a role of servitude. Shem was to father a chosen race with a special relationship with God. Jesus Christ descended, after the flesh, from the line of Shem. The name Japheth means *"enlargement"* so that God's statement of him was actually a play on words. His descendants were to encompass the globe. The following chart clearly shows how Noah's three sons replenished the Earth.

SONS	NATIONALITIES	SETTLEMENT
JAPHETH		
Gomer	Russians, Germans, Britons	Asia Minor
Magog	Scythians	Armenia
Madai	Medes	Caucasus and
Javan	Ionians, Greeks, Italians	Europe
Tubal	Iberians	
Meshech	Muscovites	
Tiras	Thracians	
HAM		
Cush	Ethiopians	Africa and
Mizraim	Egyptians	Arabia
Phut	Libyans	
Canaan	Canaanites	
SHEM		
Elam	Persians	Assyria
Asshur	Assyrians	Syria
Arphaxad	Chaldeans (Israelites)	Persia
Lud	Lydians	Northern Arabia
Aram	Armenians, Syrians	and Mesopotamia

In general, it may be stated that Japheth's descendants settled in northern, western, and eastern Europe and in Asia; Ham's descendants settled in Africa; and Shem's descendants settled in the countries surrounding Palestine.

Following the Flood, Noah lived another 350 years and died at the age of 950 (Gen. 9:28-29). This the Scripture truly stated:

"And the sons of Noah, who went forth of the Ark, were Shem, and Ham, and Japheth: and Ham is the father of Canaan. These are the three sons of Noah: AND OF THEM WAS THE WHOLE EARTH OVERSPREAD. These are the families of the sons of Noah, after their generations, in their nations: AND BY THESE WERE THE NATIONS DIVIDED IN THE EARTH AFTER THE FLOOD" (Gen. 9:18-19; 10:32).

NIMROD, THE MIGHTY HUNTER

We come now to the story of the Tower of Babel. A descendant of Ham, Nimrod, played a prominent role, for he sought to build a world empire:

"And Cush begat NIMROD: HE BEGAN TO BE A MIGHTY ONE IN THE EARTH. HE WAS A MIGHTY HUNTER BEFORE THE LORD: wherefore it is said, Even as Nimrod the mighty hunter before the LORD. And THE BEGINNING OF HIS KINGDOM WAS BABEL, and Erech, and Accad, and Calneh, in the land of Shinar" (Gen. 10:8-10).

Archaeologists have identified Nimrod, with Bacchus, Tammuz, and Adonis. Semiramis, the wife of Nimrod, has been linked to the nature goddess Rhea, Cybele, Aphrodite of Greece, and Venus of Rome. The fame of her beauty still lives in the ancient history.

Nimrod became the first leader of human apostasy and open rebellion against God since Lucifer. All religious systems of idolatry and pagan mythology have an underlying unity of character that points to their common origin in Babylon and to Nimrod its first ruler.

Nimrod was thought to be a noble friend of society because of his great hunting abilities. He slew many of the wild beasts that threatened lives and built walls to provide further protection for the cities. After the Flood the people had a holy fear of God, but Nimrod was instrumental in tearing down this trust and diverting their attention away from God, to himself.

MYSTERY RELIGIONS OF BABYLON

Nimrod was torn to pieces by a wild boar, and after his death was deified by the people. Semiramis blasphemously proclaimed that her husband had been the promised seed of Genesis 3:15 and that his death had been a voluntary sacrifice for the people!

The worship of Nimrod, under various names, developed into the mystery religions of Babylon. All knowledge was monopolized by the priesthood which had various levels, the highest being the chief priest, or Pontifex Maximus.

Because the Chaldeans believed in reincarnation, it was later accepted that Nimrod had reappeared as the supernaturally born son of his widow! It was not long before the worship of Nimrod had been replaced by the worship of the mother and the child.

This continued as Isis and Horus in Egypt, Aphrodite and Eros in Greece, Venus and Cupid in Italy, and culminated in the Roman veneration of the Virgin Mary and her son. Whereas Semiramis had been called *"the queen of heaven,"* Mary became known as *"the mother of God"*! Many of the so-called Christian festivals such as Lady Day, Easter, and Lent began in the religious system of Babylon, along with other modern rituals such as the rosary, the order of monks and nuns, holy water, and purgatorial purification after death.

Nimrod, whose name means *"the rebel,"* actually foreshadowed the coming Antichrist in many of his actions. Nimrod sought to create a world confederacy that would rebel against God and His Ways. The Antichrist also will *strive* to rule the world and bring its kingdoms into rebellion against God. Nimrod failed in this mission as will the Antichrist. Nimrod made his headquarters in Babylon, the place from which the Antichrist will rule for the first three and one-half years of his reign. Nimrod founded the religious systems of Babylon, with which the Antichrist will be associated in the last days.

TOWER OF BABEL

The building of the Tower of Babel was actually an attempt to thwart God's Plan for man to replenish and populate the whole Earth:

"And they said, Go to, let us build us a city and a tower, whose top may reach unto Heaven; and let us make us a name, LEST WE BE SCATTERED ABROAD UPON THE FACE OF THE WHOLE EARTH" (Gen. 11:4).

A description of the tower was discovered over 100 years ago. According to this Babylonian description, there was an outer court 900 feet by 1,156 feet and an inner court 450 feet by 1,056 feet. There were six gates that surrounded the courts, and a platform with encircling walls and four gates on each side. Within stood a large building about 200 feet square. Around the base of the tower were many small shrines or chapels dedicated to various gods. In the center of these buildings stood the tower itself in stages that decreased from the lowest upward, each being square. The total height of the tower was 300 feet, the same as the breadth of its base.

The building of the tower did not get the attention of God as much as did the *reason* for its building. When God perceived their motives, it is recorded:

"And THE LORD CAME DOWN to see the city and the tower, which the children of men built. And the LORD said, Behold the people is one, and they have all one language; and this they begin to do: and now nothing will be restrained from them, which they have imagined to do. Go to, LET US (the entire Trinity) *GO DOWN, AND THERE CONFOUND THEIR LANGUAGE, that they may not understand one*

another's speech" (Gen. 11:5-7).

CONFUSION OF LANGUAGES

Initially God the Father came down to Earth to view what was being accomplished against His Will. He then reported what He saw, and all three Persons of the Godhead came down to the Earth to bring Judgment upon the people. This incident is recorded in one ancient Babylonian tablet that reads:

"The building of this illustrious tower offended the gods. In a night they threw down what they had built. They scattered them abroad, and made strange their speech. Their progress was impeded. They wept hot tears for Babylon."

After the language of the people was confused, universal communication was impossible; therefore, those who spoke one language sought out others of the same dialect, and they settled in the various parts of the world, as God originally had planned.

DISTINCTION BETWEEN BABEL AND PENTECOST

This confusion of tongues continued until God once again came down through the Person of the mighty Holy Spirit on the Day of Pentecost as recorded in Acts 2. Isaiah had prophesied some 700 years previously:

"For with STAMMERING LIPS and ANOTHER TONGUE will He speak to this people. To whom He said, THIS IS THE REST wherewith you may cause the weary to rest; and THIS IS THE REFRESHING: yet they would not hear" (Isa. 28:11-12).

The Holy Spirit enabled the 120 who had gathered in the upper room to proclaim the glorious Message of God's Grace in languages that could be understood by the listeners. God's Mercy broke through the barrier that man's pride and folly had caused to be erected at Babel, in order that every man might hear and understand the glad tidings of Salvation — *"the wonderful Works of God"* (Acts 2:11).

What was God's Purpose in speaking through these individuals in other Tongues? It was to give man, in reality, one language, one hope, one object, one life! It was to gather men in such a way that they never should be scattered or confounded again! It was to give them a name and a place that would endure forever! It was to build for them a tower and a city that not only would reach to Heaven, but would have its very foundation in Heaven! This mighty Baptism with the Holy Spirit gathered them around the glorious Person of a risen and highly exalted Christ and united them all in one grand chorus of magnifying and adoring Him!

In the Book of Revelation we read:

"After this I beheld, and, lo, a great multitude, which no man could number, of all NATIONS, and KINDREDS, and PEOPLE, and TONGUES, stood before the Throne, and before the Lamb, clothed with white robes, and palms in their hands; And CRIED WITH A LOUD VOICE, saying, SALVATION TO OUR GOD WHICH SITS UPON THE THRONE, AND UNTO THE LAMB" (Rev. 7:9-10).

Thus, there are three accounts of other Tongues used in Scripture. In Genesis, Chapter 11, God gave various Tongues as an expression of His *Judgment.* In Acts, Chapter 2, He gave various Tongues as an expression of His *Grace.* In Revelation, Chapter 7, we see various Tongues gathered around the Throne of God in an expression of His *Glory!*

It is obvious that Babel ended in confusion, but Pentecost ends in glory! Babel was empowered by the spirit of fallen man, but Pentecost was endued with the Power of the Holy Spirit! Babel was the result of man exalting man, but Pentecost was the result of man exalting the Lord Jesus Christ! May the Lord help us, by the Power of the Holy Spirit, to magnify His Power, and thus be weaned from the spirit and principles of Babylon that are encroaching upon the Church even today!

DIVINE DIVISION OF CONTINENTS

The confusion of the languages at the Tower of Babel occurred before God split the Earth into continents and islands, during the days of Peleg (Gen. 10:25). Before this the whole human race was of one language and was centralized in one place on the Earth, which was one great land mass (Gen. 11:1). Following the scattering of the various language groups, the continents were divided. This explains how all of the races were brought into being, on the different continents and islands of the globe. God clearly saw the He could no longer deal with mankind as a whole, so He began to deal with a particular race called forth from Abraham. This began a new Dispensation to be discussed in the next Chapter.

DIVINE PURPOSE IN THIS DISPENSATION

The Purpose of God in the Dispensation of Human Government was to allow man to prove his faithfulness to the Lord through keeping the Laws given by God through human administration. The Laws were proposed and government established so that man could rule himself, under God's Guidance, throughout all of the ages to come. Man, of course, failed in this Dispensation as he had in the former two. The events of this period show the futility of human government that forgets God!

This is a sobering lesson to be learned in our day. When laws are passed forbidding our children to pray in public schools, when the Supreme Court sanctions the murder of untold millions of unborn babies each year, once again we catch a glimpse of the confusion that followed Babel, and the Judgment that fell on a civilization that chose to forget their God!

Chapter 8

The Dispensation Of Promise

CHAPTER EIGHT

THE DISPENSATION OF PROMISE

DEFINITION OF DISPENSATION OF PROMISE

The Book of Genesis is a book of *"beginnings."* In Genesis, Chapter 1, we read of the beginning of the Universe and the beginning of the human race with Adam and Eve. In Genesis, Chapter 8, we read of a new beginning with Noah and his family. And then in Genesis, Chapter 12, we have the beginning of God's chosen Nation in Abram. This period is called the Dispensation of Promise because of the Covenant God made with Abram:

"Now the Lord had said unto Abram, Get thee out of your country, and from your kindred, and from your father's house, unto a land that I will show you: And I will make of you a great nation, and I will bless you, and make your name great; and you shall be a blessing: And I will bless them who bless you, and curse him who curses you: and IN YOU SHALL ALL FAMILIES OF THE EARTH BE BLESSED" (Gen. 12:1-3).

These Promises, along with some 40 others, formed the basis of God's dealings with His chosen People during this period:

1. Abram was to father a great nation;
2. Abram was to be blessed;
3. Abram's name was to be made great (it was later changed to Abraham);
4. Not only would Abram be blessed, but he would be a blessing to others;
5. God would bless those who blessed Abram;
6. God would curse those who cursed Abram; and,
7. All of the families of the Earth would be blessed because of Abram's seed.

CALL OF ABRAM

This was the first time in history that God had dealt with a particular lineage separate from the rest of humanity. Because of the prevalence of idolatry and polytheism brought about by Nimrod and the religious system of Babylon, God chose to separate unto Himself one family, that through them the worship of the One True God would continue.

Through Abram would come the Nation of Israel and the promised

Messiah. This is the significance of the Promise, *"IN YOU shall all families of the Earth be blessed."* Although God had promised a Redeemer to Adam and Eve through the *"Seed"* of the woman (Gen. 3:15) and revealed that the line of Seth would be blessed in a special way (Gen. 9:26), it was not until the Call of Abram that God prophesied that Christ would come through a particular race and would bless all the nations of the Earth (Gen. 12:3).

This Prophecy will find its fulfillment during the Millennium and the eternal ages when Israel will become the leading nation of the Earth (Deut. 28:9-13; Zech. 8:23). Many of the Promises God made during the 430 years of this Dispensation will be fulfilled eternally (Gen. 17:7-8, 19; 22:17-18; etc.).

LENGTH OF THIS DISPENSATION

As stated twice in the Scriptures the Dispensation of Promise lasted 430 years:

"Now the sojourning of the Children of Israel, who dwelt in Egypt, was four hundred and thirty years" (Ex. 12:40).

"The Covenant, that was confirmed before of God in Christ, the Law, which was four hundred and thirty years after, cannot disannul, that it should make the Promise of none effect" (Gal. 3:17).

The 430 years is calculated from the Call of Abram to the Exodus of the Children of Israel from Egypt under the leadership of Moses. This time span also can be figured as follows:

25	years from Abram's Call to Isaac's birth (Gen. 12:4; 21:5)
60	years from Isaac's birth to Jacob's birth (Gen. 25:26)
147	years from Jacob's birth to his death (Gen. 47:28)
54	years from Jacob's death to Joseph's death (Gen. 37:2; 41:46; 47:28; 50:22)
<u>144</u>	years from Joseph's death to the Exodus (Ex. 12:40)
430	years from Abram's Call to the Exodus

UR OF THE CHALDEES

It was during the life of Abram that secular history began to correlate with Biblical history. We know much of the homeland of Abram, Ur of the Chaldees, from modern excavation. Houses were made of brick and actually were painted white for aesthetic purposes. Most of the homes were two stories high. The larger houses had from 10 to 20 rooms, with fully equipped kitchens, a good plumbing system, and sanitation.

There also were schools in the city of Abram's childhood. Clay tablets have been discovered that indicate some of the subjects taught in these schools. Students had writing lessons and studied the vocabulary. In arithmetic they had multiplication and division tables. More advanced scholars studied geometry, along with square roots and cubic roots. Grammar lessons included paradigms of the conjunction of verbs. This substantiates the fact that Abram came from a city of high civilization that existed about 2000 B.C.

Idolatry was the religious system of Abram's day. There was family worship of household gods, and each home had an altar that displayed clay figurines of these gods, which were called *"teraphim."* These family gods served as *"guardian angels"* of the home. When the father died, these idols often were left to the oldest son so that the worship could continue. The teraphim are mentioned in connection with Laban and Rachel:

"And Laban went to shear his sheep: and Rachel had stolen THE IMAGES that were her father's. And now, though you would need be gone, because you sore longed after your father's house, yet wherefore have you stolen MY GODS? Now Rachel had taken THE IMAGES, and put them in the camel's furniture, and sat upon them. And Laban searched all the tent, but found them not" (Gen. 31:19, 30, 34).

The possession of the household gods was the equivalent of having the family inheritance; therefore, Rachel sought to steal her brother's birthright so that Jacob could be the legal heir!

Abram did not involve himself or his family in the idolatrous worship of his society. After he left Ur, as God had commanded, along with Sarai (who later became Sarah), his wife, and Lot, his nephew, and along with their servants, Abram built an Altar unto the Lord in Sichem, in the Plain of Moreh. The Lord appeared again to Abram in Sichem (Shechem):

"And the Lord appeared unto Abram, and said, Unto your seed will I give this land" (Gen. 12:7).

PROMISED LAND

Again the Covenant was confirmed that God was going to raise up a nation from Abram and give to them the land of Canaan. The Scripture also declares that *"the Canaanite was then in the land"* (Gen. 12:6). The Canaanites were part of the giant races that appeared both before and *after* the Flood (Gen. 6:4). Satan still intended to corrupt the human race with the mingling of the fallen Angels and the *"daughters of men,"* so that the *"Seed"* of the woman could not be born. The giants possessed Canaan and the surrounding countries, but God allowed Israel to multiply in Egypt until they became strong enough to kill these giants and possess their land.

Satan delights in robbing God's Children of their rights and privileges. He uses a variety of methods to get people to doubt God's Word. He uses fear to combat the Faith of the Believer. He uses circumstances to bring about difficulties in the life of individuals, so that God's Will cannot be performed in their life.

It is Satan's will to bring doubt, when it is God's Will to build Faith! It is Satan's will to bring sickness, when it is God's Will to bring healing! It is Satan's will to bring failure, when it is God's Will for His Children to prosper! It was Satan's will to keep the Children of Israel out of the Promised Land, but it was God's Will for them to possess the land! And they did!

TEST OF THIS DISPENSATION

The only test for man in this Dispensation was to *believe* God's Promises and to live by the Covenant given to Abram. Men were expected, of course, to obey all of the civil laws that did not oppose God's Will for them, as well. Man, in general, had knowledge of the True God through the witness of Abram and Melchizedek, the king of Salem (Gen. 14:18), in addition to Isaac, Jacob, and others throughout this age. Man was without excuse for not serving God and believing His Word.

DIVINE PURPOSE IN THIS DISPENSATION

God purposed in the Dispensation of Promise to make Abram and his family His witnesses in the Earth. He desired to bless them spiritually, physically, and financially. God wanted to show the heathen nations the Blessings of serving the Living and True God, and the utter futility of worshiping dumb idols. The Blessings of Salvation that we now enjoy were made available through the Covenant God made with Abram. These include Faith, Remission of sin, Justification, Sanctification, bodily Healing, answers to prayer, Spiritual Revelations, etc. All these wonderful gifts could also be received in the Dispensation of Promise by simply trusting God's Word!

Abram left Sichem and pitched his tent toward Bethel, which means *"house of God."* There he built another Altar unto the Lord and worshiped. When a famine struck the land, Abram continued his journey and *"went down"* into Egypt (Gen. 12:10). His going down typified his failure, for he was to remain in the land.

Because he feared that the Egyptians would kill him and take his wife, Abram commanded Sarai to tell the Egyptians that she was his *"sister"* (Gen. 12:11-13). This was not a total lie, for Sarai was his half sister (Gen. 20:12). The sin was Abram's failure to believe that God would protect both himself and Sarai. He should have realized that the Egyptians could not have killed him, for he had no seed as yet, and God was bound to keep His Promise to Abram!

As is always the case, *"your sin will find you out"* (Num. 32:23). Pharaoh discovered that Sarai was his wife, and commanded her and Abram to depart (Gen. 12:14-20).

Therefore, Abram *"went up"* out of Egypt, and it is recorded that he was *"very rich in cattle, in silver, and in gold"* (Gen. 13:2). It is so very important for all of God's People to move only in the Perfect Will of God in order to maintain God's Blessings.

SEPARATION BETWEEN ABRAM AND LOT

It had been many years since the Call of Abram and God's Covenant with him. Still the Promise had not come to pass. Abram did not have a great name. There was no great Nation, not even a son!

Why? It may have been due to Abram's incomplete obedience to the command *"get you out of your country, AND FROM YOUR KIN-DRED"* (Gen. 12:1). And so Abram returned to Bethel and *"called on the Name of the LORD"* (Gen. 13:4); and, no doubt, he repented for his doubt and unbelief.

It was at this point that Abram almost was forced to obey fully the Command of the Lord to separate from his kindred, for the land had become too small for Abram and Lot to dwell together with all of their flocks, herds, tents, and possessions (Gen. 13:5-7). The Canaanites and the Perizzites (giant races) also were dwelling in the land.

Therefore, Abram and his nephew decided to part from one another. Abram gave Lot the first choice of the land. Lot chose the Plain of Jordan, and *"pitched his tent toward Sodom"* and the cities of the plain. Abram dwelled in the land of Canaan (Gen. 13:8-12). After Abram fully obeyed the Lord, God confirmed His Covenant once again with him:

"And the Lord said unto Abram, AFTER that Lot was separated from him, Lift up now your eyes, and look from the place where you are northward, and southward, and eastward, and westward: FOR ALL THE LAND WHICH YOU SEE, TO YOU WILL I GIVE IT, AND TO YOUR SEED FOR EVER. AND I WILL MAKE YOUR SEED AS THE DUST OF THE EARTH: so that if a man can number the dust of the Earth, then shall your seed also be numbered. ARISE, WALK THROUGH THE LAND IN THE LENGTH OF IT AND IN THE BREADTH OF IT;

FOR I WILL GIVE IT UNTO YOU" (Gen. 13:14-17).

CONDITIONAL PROMISES OF GOD

All of the Promises of God are *conditional*. If we do *our* part, God will always do *His* part. When two people enter into a contract or an agreement, there are terms to be met by both parties. Notice how this is true also of God's Promises.

1. SALVATION

"That if YOU shall confess with YOUR mouth the Lord Jesus, and shall believe in your heart that God has raised Him from the dead, you shall be Saved" (Rom. 10:9).

MAN confesses and believes and *GOD* saves him!

2. HOLY SPIRIT BAPTISM

"Men and brethren, what shall WE do? Then Peter said unto them, Repent, and be baptized every one of YOU in the Name of Jesus Christ for the Remission of sins, and YOU shall receive the Gift of the Holy Spirit" (Acts 2:37-38).

MAN repents and obeys the Lord, and *GOD* fills him with the Spirit!

3. BODILY HEALING

"Is any sick among YOU? let HIM call for the Elders of the Church; and let them pray over him, anointing him with oil in the Name of the Lord: And the prayer of Faith shall save the sick, and THE LORD shall raise him up" (James 5:14-15).

MAN calls for the Elders to anoint him with oil and pray the prayer of Faith, and *GOD* heals his body!

4. ANSWERS TO PRAYER

"Therefore I say unto YOU, What things soever YOU desire, when YOU pray, believe that you receive them, and you shall have them" (Mk. 11:24).

MAN prays in Faith, believing, and *GOD* answers his prayer! We could go on and on with all of the other Promises of God: forgiveness (I Jn. 1:9), prosperity (Josh. 1:8), daily provision (Mat. 6:33), Salvation of lost loved ones (Acts 16:31), wisdom (James 1:5), Gifts of the Spirit (I Cor. 12), and whatever else we need from God (Mk. 9:23)!

After Abram separated from Lot, he dwelt in the Plain of Mamre, in Hebron, *"and built there an Altar unto the LORD"* (Gen. 13:18). Abram, no doubt, spent time on his knees repenting for his delay in fully obeying the Lord, and God once again blessed him, for he was given the victory over the enemy soldiers that had captured Lot and his people (Gen. 14:1-16). Out of a thankful heart, Melchizedek, the king of Salem, who was also *"the Priest of the Most High God"* (Gen. 14:18), brought forth some bread and wine (symbols of the Atonement) and blessed Abram.

PRINCIPLE OF TITHING

Abram gave the Priest a tenth of *ALL* the spoil of the battle (Gen. 14:20). This is the first recorded instance of paying tithes unto the Lord. Those who argue that tithing was practiced only under the Law of Moses are unscriptural, for Abram tithed a few hundred years before the Law was even given! Jesus commanded tithing during the Dispensation of Grace as well (Mat. 23:23), for the Dispensation of Law lasted only until John the Baptist (Lk. 16:16), as we shall discuss in the next chapter.

Even as Abram gave *ALL* the tithe unto God and was blessed, those who give one-tenth of their income along with special offerings unto the Lord are promised untold blessings.

"Bring ye ALL the tithes into the storehouse, that there may be meat in My House, and prove Me now herewith, saith the LORD of Hosts, if I will not OPEN YOU THE WINDOWS OF HEAVEN, AND POUR YOU OUT A BLESSING, THAT THERE SHALL NOT BE ROOM ENOUGH TO RECEIVE IT" (Mal. 3:10).

Those who refuse to give tithes and give to the Work of the Lord are placed under a curse (Mal. 3:8-9) and never will be *fully* blessed of the Lord.

After Abram paid his tithes, God appeared to him once again in a vision, and confirmed that he would indeed have a son. Abram had begun to believe that his servant Eliezer might become the promised heir. But God showed Abram that *He* was his shield and exceeding great reward (Gen. 5:1). It was unnecessary for Abram to look to the natural realm for fulfillment of His Promise to him:

"And, behold, the Word of the LORD came unto him, saying, This shall not be your heir; but he who shall come forth out of your own bowels shall be your heir. And He brought him forth abroad, and said, Look now toward Heaven, and tell the stars, if you be able to number them: and He said unto him, SO SHALL YOUR SEED BE" (Gen. 15:4-5).

Israel never did possess fully the land as God described, so this must have future fulfillment in the Millennium (Ezek. 47:13 through 48:29).

DESCRIPTION OF GIANTS IN CANAAN

All of the Tribes mentioned in Genesis 15:19-21, once again, refer to the giant races that inhabited the land God intended for Abram and his seed. The *Rephaims* mentioned in Genesis 14:5 and 15:20 were also giants. In fact, the word is translated *"giants"* in several Scriptures (Deut. 2:11; 3:11; Josh. 12:4; 17:15; II Sam. 21:22; I Chron. 20:4; *et al*).

One of the last surviving members of the Tribe of Rephaim was Og, the king of Bashan, who stood nearly 13 feet tall! His bedstead was a bedstead of iron and measured 13 ½ feet long by 6 feet wide (Deut. 3:11)! His kingdom of Bashan was also called *"the land of giants"* (Deut. 3:13).

Argob, one of the cities of Bashan, was known as *"the land of sacred romance,"* which has obvious reference to the cohabitation of the sons of God (fallen Angels) with the daughters of men, whose offspring became the giant races (Gen. 6:4).

The remains of ancient Bashan show that the houses were constructed mainly of marble, with ceilings and doors measuring from 10 to 30 feet high! Goliath, whom David killed, stood over 9 feet tall, and his coat of armor weighed 125 pounds (I Sam. 17:4-6)! The forces of David later killed the remaining giants (II Sam. 21:22), one of whom was described as being of great stature and as having six fingers on both hands and six toes on both feet (II Sam. 21:20)!

It is possible that the pyramids of Egypt, the giant cities of Bashan, and other huge monuments were the result of the labor and skill of these giant creatures. If not, their origin remains a puzzling mystery. These giant races caused the Israelites continual struggle until finally they were killed.

BIRTH OF ISHMAEL

After 15 years had passed, Abram and Sarai still did not have the son God had promised them. Therefore, Sarai sought to assist God by suggesting that Abram take her maid, Hagar, to be his wife and bear him a son (Gen. 16:1-3). This was legal, for according to civil law the children of slaves belonged to the master.

After Hagar conceived, Sarai was angry (and probably jealous) that the events had come to pass. Because the law would not permit Sarai to sell Hagar under such circumstances, she *"dealt hardly with her,"* making her life so miserable that she finally fled (Gen. 16:4-8).

"The Angel of the LORD" (who was the preincarnate Christ) appeared to Hagar and commanded her to return to Sarai and to submit herself under her hands, for He said:

"I will multiply your seed exceedingly, that it shall not be numbered for multitude. And the Angel of the LORD said unto her, Behold, you are with child, and you shall bear a son, and shall call his name

Ishmael; because the LORD has heard your affliction. And he will be a wild man; his hand will be against every man, and every man's hand against him; and he shall dwell in the presence of all his brethren" (Gen. 16:10-12).

The Lord told Hagar that her son also would father a great nation. The characteristics that were given concerning Ishmael were certainly true of himself, but also have been true of his descendants, the Arabs, throughout history and even today!

It was not God's Plan for Abram to obtain the Promised son in this manner, and it brought about trouble and sorrow for the entire family. Abram was 86 years of age when Ishmael was born (Gen. 16:16), and after 13 *more* years he *still* did not have the Promised son!

"And when Abram was ninety years old and nine, the Lord appeared to Abram, and said unto him, I am the Almighty God; walk before Me, and be thou perfect" (Gen. 17:1).

EL SHADDAI — THE ALMIGHTY

This is the first reference of God revealing Himself as *El Shaddai*, the Almighty God. This revelation was well suited for the occasion, for only a God of miracles could meet Abram's need at this time. With Abram at the age of 99, and his wife at the age of 89, both beyond the years of child-bearing, it seemed impossible that they still could have hoped for a son. *"With men it is impossible, but not with God: for WITH GOD ALL THINGS ARE POSSIBLE"* (Mk. 10:27). He is *El Shaddai*, the All-sufficient One!

The Apostle Paul described the Faith of Abraham:

"(As it is written, I have made you a father of many nations,) before Him Whom he believed, even God, who quickens the dead, and CALLS THOSE THINGS WHICH BE NOT AS THOUGH THEY WERE. Who against hope believed in hope, that he might become the father of many nations; according to that which was spoken, So shall your seed be. And being not weak in Faith, he considered not his own body NOW DEAD, when he was about an hundred years old, neither yet the DEADNESS of Sarah's womb: HE STAGGERED NOT AT THE PROMISE OF GOD THROUGH UNBELIEF; BUT WAS STRONG IN FAITH, GIVING GLORY TO GOD; And being fully persuaded that, WHAT HE HAD PROMISED, HE WAS ABLE ALSO TO PERFORM" (Rom. 4:17-21).

NEW NAMES FOR ABRAM AND SARAI

It was during this fifth appearance of the Lord to Abram that God once again confirmed the Promises that He had made many years before (Gen. 17:1-8). God also changed the names of Abram and Sarai to Abraham and Sarah. The name Abram meant *"exalted father,"* whereas the name Abraham meant *"father of a multitude"*! The name Sarah meant *"princess"* (Gen. 17:5-15).

COVENANT OF CIRCUMCISION

God also gave to Abraham the sign of the Covenant, which was circumcision (Gen. 17:11). This practice was to continue forever as a continual reminder of God's Promise to Israel. God felt so strongly about this command that He instituted the death penalty for any who refused to obey (Gen. 17:14).

God also reminded Abraham that although He had a plan for Ishmael (Gen. 17:20), Sarah indeed would bear a son, and he was to call his name Isaac. God would establish His Covenant through Isaac and his seed *forever* (Gen. 17:19). God even specified the time that Isaac would be born — *"this set time in the next year"* (Gen. 17:21).

Some would question why God did not reveal *all* of His Plan to Abraham in the beginning, but allowed Abraham and Sarah to continue for several years without the full knowledge or the fulfillment of the Promise. God's timing is so very important! It seems that God delights in answering prayer or fulfilling a promise just *"in the nick of time"*!

Someone humorously has stated that God never has been *late* with the answer to a prayer, but He has missed several opportunities to be *early*!

Even when God gave His Son as the Redeemer of mankind, it was *"when the FULNESS of the time was come"* (Gal. 4:4). Although God had His timing also in dealing with Abraham and Sarah, He, no doubt, wanted to test their Faith and their ability to believe the Promises of God, for this *was* the one test of the Dispensation of Promise.

CONFIRMATION OF THE PROMISE

After Abraham obeyed the Lord in circumcising both himself and Ishmael, who was now 13 years old, along with all the men in his household (Gen. 17:26-27), God once again appeared to him, this time with three Angels (Gen. 18:1-2).

God and the Angels had the appearance of *men*. Abraham washed their feet, killed a calf, Sarah cooked dinner for them, and *"they did eat"* (Gen. 18:1-8).

The Lord reminded Abraham that Sarah would have a son. Sarah, who overheard what was being said, snickered at the thought of a 90-year-old woman having a baby. God heard Sarah laugh and spoke these tremendous words, *"IS ANY THING TOO HARD FOR THE LORD?"* (Gen. 18:9-15).

DESTRUCTION OF SODOM AND GOMORRAH

The Lord also told Abraham that He and the Angels had come down to the Earth to destroy the cities of the plain, Sodom and Gomorrah, because *"their sin is very grievous"* (Gen. 18:20). The sin of homosexuality has never been tolerated by God, and always has brought the severest Judgment of the Lord. Even today God will not tolerate this abomination that is spreading across our land.

Abraham begged the Lord to spare the cities, for he loved his nephew, Lot. God replied that if He could find just 10 righteous people in Sodom and Gomorrah, He would not destroy them. Although God did spare the life of Lot and his family, there were no other righteous people to be found.

The wickedness of Sodom and Gomorrah was so abominable, that the men of the city actually tried to assault the two Angels of the Lord. Even after the Angels smote them with blindness, the Sodomites were so persistent in their vile and perverted lust that they *"wearied themselves to find the door"* so that they could attempt to commit their horrible acts with the men inside (Gen. 19:1-11).

The Angels rescued Lot, his wife, and their two daughters just in time for them to escape the destruction of the cities with fire and brimstone (Gen. 19:23-25). Lot's wife, whose heart was still in Sodom, disobeyed the Lord, looked back toward the city, and became a pillar of salt.

Lot suffered miserably for *"pitch*(ing) *his tent toward Sodom"* (Gen. 13:12), for even his daughters were corrupted by the loose morals of that wicked society and committed incest with their father after making him drunk (Gen. 19:33-38)! This is the sad record of a family torn by the ravages of sin!

BIRTH OF ISAAC

Fourteen years after the birth of Ishmael, Sarah gave birth to the son God had promised, Isaac, which means *"laughter."* Abraham prepared a feast on the day that Isaac was weaned, and Sarah saw Ishmael mocking and making fun of them. Therefore, she insisted that Abraham cast out Hagar and her son. God comforted Abraham, reminding him that He indeed would make of Ishmael a great nation, but through Isaac would

Abraham's *"seed be called"* (Gen. 21:1-12).

NATIONS OF ISAAC AND ISHMAEL

From the very beginning Ishmael and Isaac were enemies, although they were sons of the same father. Their descendants, the Arabs and the Jews, have remained enemies even to this day! The Arabs claim the land of Palestine due to Ishmael being the firstborn son of Abraham. The Jews claim the land due to the Covenant God made with Abraham. This rivalry will continue until God sets His People permanently in the land of their possession (Isa. 11:11-16).

SUPREME TEST OF ABRAHAM'S FAITH

The supreme test for Abraham came when God commanded him to offer his son Isaac as a sacrifice before the Lord. The Faith of Abraham is manifested in the words he spoke both to his servants and to Isaac himself. To his servants Abraham said:

"Abide you here with the ass; and I and the lad will go yonder and worship, AND COME AGAIN TO YOU" (Gen. 22:5).

The most difficult part of this test must have come when Isaac asked:

"Behold the fire and the wood: but where is the lamb for a Burnt Offering?" (Gen. 22:7).

Abraham answered his son with words of Faith:

"My son, GOD WILL PROVIDE HIMSELF A LAMB FOR A BURNT OFFERING" (Gen. 22:8).

The Book of Hebrews explains that by Faith Abraham reckoned *"... that God was able to raise him up, even from the dead; from whence also he received him in a figure"* (Heb. 11:19).

JEHOVAH-JIREH — THE LORD WILL PROVIDE

This total and complete obedience was rewarded by the Lord. For when Abraham tied Isaac to the Altar and drew back the knife to slay his son, the Angel of the Lord called unto him from Heaven and said:

"Lay not your hand upon the lad, neither do you any thing unto him: FOR NOW I KNOW THAT YOU FEAR GOD, SEEING YOU HAVE NOT WITHHELD YOUR SON, YOUR ONLY SON FROM ME" (Gen. 22:12).

God provided a ram for them to sacrifice, and what a time of worship they must have had! Abraham called the place *Jehovah-jireh*, which means *"the Lord will provide."*

ISAAC'S TWO SONS

Isaac had twin sons and named them Esau and Jacob. Esau, who was the firstborn son, foolishly sold his birthright to Jacob (Gen. 25:27-34). After a life of deception and fraud, Jacob had a change of heart, and learned total dependence upon the Lord. God changed his name from Jacob, which meant *"deceiver,"* to Israel, which meant *"prince of God"* (Gen. 32:24-32).

JACOB'S TWELVE SONS

Jacob had 12 sons from whom came the Twelve Tribes of Israel: Reuben, Simeon, Levi, Judah, Issachar, Zebulun, Joseph, Benjamin, Dan, Naphtali, Gad, and Asher (Gen. 35:23-26). It seems there was a lessening of spiritual values from Abraham to Isaac and from Isaac to Jacob, but even more so from Jacob to his 12 sons. Still Joseph maintained his integrity before God. Because of its purity, Joseph's exemplary life has been compared to that of Christ.

JOSEPH'S FAITHFULNESS

Because of the jealousy in their heart toward Joseph, some of the brothers plotted to kill him and sold him into Egyptian bondage (Gen. 37:11-34). Thirteen years later there was a famine in the land, and all the people came to Egypt to obtain food (Gen. 41:57). All of Jacob's household, 66 of them, came to Egypt where they discovered that Joseph was the prime minister (Gen. 46:27-34). God's Blessings rested upon Joseph because of his Faithfulness to Him.

EGYPTIAN BONDAGE

Shortly thereafter Jacob died. Fifty-four years later Joseph died also, and a Pharaoh *"which knew not Joseph"* (Ex. 1:8) came to the throne. This Pharaoh discovered that the Children of Israel were stronger and mightier than the Egyptians, for there were about 2,000,000 Israelites by this time. Fearing that the Children of Israel would cause a national upheaval and bring his throne into jeopardy, the Pharaoh issued a cruel decree that all of the male Hebrew babies should be thrown into the river. Moses was born during this time, and was hidden by his mother in the bulrushes (Ex. 2:1-10). Pharaoh's daughter found him and had compassion on him. Moses was reared in Pharaoh's palace and received the finest education. God was preparing him for a specific task (Acts 7:20-22).

CALL OF MOSES AND THE EXODUS

Life for the Children of Israel was extremely difficult, for they lived as Egyptian slaves. The Purpose of God in allowing them to go into Egypt was twofold: (1) to judge them for their rebellion and (2) to allow them to multiply and become a great nation. When this was accomplished, the Children of Israel cried unto the Lord for deliverance! The Scripture declares:

"And God heard their groaning, and God remembered His Covenant with Abraham, with Isaac, and with Jacob. And God looked upon the Children of Israel, and God had respect unto them" (Ex. 2:24-25).

It was at this point that God called Moses to lead the Nation of Israel out of Egyptian bondage (Ex. 3:1-12). Moses went before the Pharaoh, with Aaron his brother, and said:

"Thus saith the LORD God of Israel, LET MY PEOPLE GO, that they may hold a feast unto Me in the wilderness" (Ex. 5:1).

Pharaoh refused to hearken to the voice of Moses as God already had prophesied. It was not until God brought a variety of Judgments upon the nation of Egypt that Pharaoh finally consented. These plagues included water turning to blood (Ex. 7:14-25), frogs (Ex. 8:1-15), lice (Ex. 8:16-19), flies (Ex. 8:24), a disease upon the cattle (Ex. 9:1-7), boils (Ex. 9:8-12), hail (Ex. 8:13-35), locusts (Ex. 10:4-15), darkness (Ex. 10:21-23), and finally the death of the firstborn (Ex. 11:4-7). The Passover was instituted by God and observed for the first time by the Children of Israel (Ex. 12:1-17). To every home that had obeyed this Commandment of the Lord, God promised:

"WHEN I SEE THE BLOOD, I WILL PASS OVER YOU" (Ex. 12:13).

That night the firstborn of all the families of Egypt was killed. It is recorded:

"There was not a house where there was not one dead" (Ex. 12:30).

When this occurred, Pharaoh commanded the Children of Israel to depart from Egypt. Although there were only 70 Israelites when they first entered Egypt, there now existed a mighty nation of over 2,000,000 men, women, and children, along with the flocks and herds, silver and gold, and all that the Egyptians had heaped upon them in their fear that God would bring more Judgment upon them (Ex. 12:33-36).

God had brought blessing out of adversity! Israel was finally free from the bondage of Egypt, and God had great plans for His People. Thus, the Dispensation of Promise ended in Judgment as the other Dispensations before. But there was also the continued Promise of a coming Redeemer Who was mighty to save!

The Covenant that God made with Abraham is just as true today as it was the day God made the Promises! God has blessed those who have blessed Israel, and He has cursed those who have mistreated Israel. The mighty defeat of Hitler's regime and the Blessings of God upon America are constant reminders that GOD KEEPS HIS PROMISES TO THOSE WHO BELIEVE!

Chapter 9

The Dispensation Of Law

Continued . . .

CHAPTER NINE

THE DISPENSATION OF LAW

GOD'S PURPOSE FOR ISRAEL

When God called Abram from Ur of the Chaldees (Gen. 11:31), He desired to create a new nation, a peculiar people, distinct from all others. The Lord wanted a Holy people, an elect race that would be a special possession to Him (Deut. 7:6). It was God's intention that Israel should be a pure theocracy both politically and religiously.

Amid a corrupt and idolatrous society, Israel, as a sanctified nation, was to display her devotion and loyalty to Jehovah — the One who had separated her unto Himself. Israel was God's chosen People, upon whom He lavished His Blessings and who were led by His continued Presence (Ex. 14:19).

GOD'S COVENANT WITH ISRAEL

God bound Himself to Israel through the Covenant He made with Abraham. It was of such great importance that God confirmed it six times to Abraham and twice to Isaac and Jacob (Gen. 12:1-3; 13:14-17; 15:1-7; 17:1-8; etc.). The seed of Abraham was symbolized by *"the stars of the heaven"* (Gen. 22:17), which spoke of a *spiritual* posterity, and *"the sand which is upon the sea shore"* (Gen. 22:17), or *"the dust of the Earth"* (Gen. 13:16), which spoke of a *physical* posterity. The Blessings of the Covenant were Spiritual as well as physical!

ETERNAL COVENANT

God's Covenant with Abraham is eternal. No provision was made for its recall! The Dispensation of Law did not revoke the provisions and Blessings of the Covenant:

"The Covenant, that was confirmed before of God in Christ, the Law, which was four hundred and thirty years after, cannot disannul, that it should make the Promises of none effect. For if the inheritance be of the Law, it is no more of Promise: but God gave it to Abraham by Promise" (Gal. 3:17-18).

The Promises are definitely *all* going to be fulfilled, and Israel is guaranteed an everlasting continuance as a nation with eternal possession of the Promised Land. Some persons have taught that the sins of Israel, primarily that of rejecting Jesus as the Messiah, have transferred the Covenant Blessings from Israel to the Church, which has become *"spiritual Israel."* In essence, this teaching states that God no longer will deal with Israel because the Covenant was broken. The Apostle Paul, however, showed clearly that God has not cast off Israel forever, but will fulfill the Covenant as He promised:

"I say then, Has God cast away His People? GOD FORBID. For I also am an Israelite, of the seed of Abraham, of the Tribe of Benjamin. GOD HAS NOT CAST AWAY HIS PEOPLE WHICH HE FOREKNEW. For I would not, Brethren, that you should be ignorant of this mystery, lest you should be wise in your own conceits; that BLINDNESS IN PART IS HAPPENED TO ISRAEL, UNTIL THE FULNESS OF THE GENTILES BE COME IN. AND SO ALL ISRAEL SHALL BE SAVED: as it is written, There shall come out of Sion the Deliverer, and shall turn away ungodliness from Jacob: FOR THIS IS MY COVENANT UNTO THEM, WHEN I SHALL TAKE AWAY THEIR SINS. As concerning the Gospel, they are enemies for your sakes: BUT AS TOUCHING THE ELECTION, THEY ARE BELOVED FOR THE FATHERS' SAKES. FOR THE GIFTS AND CALLING OF GOD ARE WITHOUT REPENTANCE" (Rom. 11:1-2, 25-29).

According to the Prophets, quoted by the Apostle Paul, Israel, regathered from all nations, restored to her own land and converted, is yet to have her greatest earthly exaltation and glory (Zech. 12:8-10; 13:1-9; Amos 9:11-15; Mic. 4:1-8; Isa. 59:20-21). The Prophet Jeremiah declared that only if the sun, moon, and stars departed, would Israel cease to be a nation (Jer. 31:35-36). Ezekiel prophesied:

"And they shall dwell in the land that I have given unto Jacob My servant, wherein your fathers have dwelt; and they shall dwell therein, even they, and their children, and their children's children FOR EVER: and My servant David shall be their prince FOR EVER" (Ezek. 37:25).

Although the moral failure of Israel as a nation has resulted in untold punishment, Israel's transgressions have not defeated the Plan of God, or permanently alienated His People from Him. God's Covenant with Abraham will be fulfilled.

LENGTH OF THIS DISPENSATION

The Dispensation of Law lasted *generally* from Moses to Jesus Christ and *specifically* from the Exodus from Egypt to the preaching of John the Baptist, the forerunner of Christ:

"For the LAW was given by MOSES, but GRACE and Truth came

by JESUS CHRIST" (Jn. 1:17).

"From the days of John the Baptist until now the Kingdom of Heaven suffers violence, and the violent take it by force. For all the Prophets, and THE LAW prophesied UNTIL JOHN" (Mat. 11:12-13).

"THE LAW and the Prophets were UNTIL JOHN: since that time the Kingdom of God is preached, and every man presses into it" (Lk. 16:16).

This period lasted for more than 1,718 years and is calculated from the following statements:

41 years from the Exodus to the entrance into Canaan

520 years (or more) from the entrance into Canaan to the reign of King Saul

513 years from King Saul to the Babylonian Captivity

164 years from the Babylonian Captivity to the Restoration

480 years from the Restoration to Christ's Ministry introduced by John the Baptist

1,718 years (or more) from Moses to Christ or from the Exodus to the preaching of John the Baptist

ISRAEL IN THE TIMES OF THE GENTILES

"The times of the Gentiles" spoken of by Jesus in Luke 21:24 began with the Egyptian bondage, discussed in the last chapter. Israel continued to be more or less dominated by Gentile nations throughout the Dispensation of Law. Following the Exodus from Egypt, the armies of Pharaoh pursued the Israelites, to bring them once again into bondage. As the Children of Israel stood helplessly before the Red Sea, God commanded Moses to lift up his rod and stretch forth his hand over the sea. When he obeyed, the waters rolled back, allowing Israel to cross on dry ground. When the last of God's People had crossed over the sea, God commanded Moses to stretch forth his hand over the sea again, and the Egyptian armies were overthrown by the waters:

"But the Children of Israel walked upon dry land in the midst of the Sea; and the waters were a wall unto them on their right hand, and on their left. Thus the Lord saved Israel that day out of the hand of the Egyptians; and Israel saw the Egyptians dead upon the sea shore" (Ex. 14:29-30).

DELIVERANCE FROM EGYPTIAN BONDAGE

With the Red Sea before them, the Egyptian armies behind them, and the mountains on either side, the Children of Israel could only look *UP* to the Lord for Deliverance. God brought a mighty Victory! They crossed the Red Sea, journeyed in the wilderness for three months, and came to Sinai where they stayed for one year and one month (Ex. 19:1-2; Num. 1:1). It was at Sinai that the Law was given, the Tabernacle was built, and the nation was organized and instructed in the Law.

Following this time, the Children of Israel left Sinai and came to Kadesh-barnea, where they rebelled against the Lord and refused to enter the Promised Land (Num. 10:11 through 14:12). Because of their rebellion, they were allowed to wander in the wilderness for 40 years (Num. 14:22-45). After the death of Moses, Joshua led Israel in conquering all the land of Canaan and taking possession of it. The land was divided east and west of Jordan into 12 parts (Josh. 3:1 through 22:34). Israel served the Lord throughout Joshua's leadership and the Elders who followed him, approximately 30 years (Josh. 14:7; 24:29).

For 450 years after this, Israel served false gods and became the servants of various nations. When the Children of Israel repented, God raised up Judges to deliver them. This cycle of Repentance and backsliding continued throughout the terms of 16 Judges, ending with Samuel (Judg. 2:7 through 16:31; I Sam. 3:21; 7:2-15).

When Israel demanded a king, God gave them Saul, who conquered their present enemies. Saul also rebelled against the Lord; therefore, David was chosen as his successor (I Sam. 11:1 through 16:13). Saul was extremely jealous of David, especially after he killed Goliath; therefore, Saul made over 20 attempts to kill David. Saul finally died after a 40-year reign (read I Sam. 17:1 through 31:13).

David ruled over the Tribe of Judah while Abner made the son of Saul, Ish-bosheth, king over the remaining 11 tribes (II Sam. 2:1-11). David later became king over all of Israel, after a reign of over seven years.

During David's reign, the city of Jerusalem was made capital of the united kingdom (II Sam. 5:6-12). His entire reign lasted 40 years, during which time he conquered all of the remaining territory to the River Euphrates (read II Sam. 8:1 through 12:31).

David failed the Lord by committing adultery with Bath-sheba and by ordering her husband, Uriah, killed (II Sam. 11:1-27). The Lord forgave him, but Nathan the Prophet told David, *"Therefore the sword shall never depart from your house"* (II Sam. 12:10). David reaped a life of heartache and misery because of his great failure.

When he grew old, David made Solomon King (I Ki. 2:1-12). Solomon's inheritance of the kingdom of Israel included the land from the Mediterranean Sea to the River Euphrates and from Egypt to Hamath. He increased the kingdom extensively, and built the first Temple in Jerusalem (I Ki. 6:1-38). Solomon's Temple was an ancient wonder, valued at more than $200 billion in modern-day estimates. Solomon's 40-year reign brought *material* prosperity to the kingdom, but lacked *spiritual* prosperity.

ASSYRIAN OPPRESSION

After Solomon's death, his son Rehoboam became king. The people of the 10 Tribes led a revolt and chose Jeroboam as their king. Thus, for the next 260 years Israel was divided into the Northern Kingdom and the Southern Kingdom.

The Northern Kingdom, which included all of the Tribes except Judah and Benjamin, established idolatry and grew increasingly wicked. God allowed various nations to oppress them until 749 B.C. when the 10 Tribes were taken into Assyrian Captivity. While Egypt was the *first* world empire to oppress Israel, Assyria became the *second* world empire to oppress Israel in *"the times of the Gentiles."* (Read I Ki. 11:41-43; I Ki. 12 through II Ki. 17.)

BABYLONIAN OPPRESSION

The kings who ruled the Southern Kingdom of Judah and Benjamin were also wicked, with the exception of Asa, Jehoshaphat, Joash, Amaziah, Uzziah, Jotham, Hezekiah, and Josiah (and even they, at times, turned from God). While the Northern Kingdom was totally idolatrous, the Southern Kingdom worshiped the Lord sporadically, although many of the people corrupted their worship with idols.

After the Northern Kingdom was taken into Assyrian Captivity, idolatry increased in the Southern Kingdom until they were taken into Babylonian Captivity. The 10 Tribes remained captives in Assyria for 203 years, and the two Tribes remained in Babylonian Captivity for 70 years.

After this a remnant of the whole 12 Tribes returned under Zerubbabel, Ezra, and Nehemiah. It was during the 133 years after the Northern Kingdom was carried into captivity and before the Southern Kingdom was carried into captivity that the Babylonian Empire conquered the Assyrian Empire and became the *third* world empire to oppress Israel in *"the times of the Gentiles."* The 10 Tribes already had been in captivity to Assyria when the two Tribes were taken into captivity by Babylon; therefore, Israel, as a whole, was captive to Babylon for 70 years (Jer. 25:1-14).

MEDO-PERSIAN OPPRESSION

Babylon then was overthrown by the Medes and Persians (Dan.

5:26-31). The Medo-Persian Empire became the *fourth* world empire to oppress Israel in *"the times of the Gentiles."* Darius, the Mede (Dan. 5:31), was followed by Cyrus, the Persian (Ezra 1:1-4), who decreed the Restoration of Israel along with their city and Temple. Isaiah had uttered this Prophecy more than 180 years before, foretelling that one who knew not God (Isa. 45:1-5) would be instrumental in setting God's People free from the Babylonian Captivity. Cyrus himself must have been startled and greatly amazed to find himself, mentioned by name, in the old Hebrew scroll, written well over a century before he even was born:

"Who says of CYRUS, He is My shepherd, and shall perform all My pleasure: even saying to Jerusalem, You shall be built; and to the Temple, Your foundation shall be laid" (Isa. 44:28).

Cyrus not only allowed the Jews to return to Jerusalem, but gave them money and materials for rebuilding the Temple. He also returned 5,400 gold and silver vessels that Nebuchadnezzar had taken from the Temple when he overthrew the city (Jer. 28:2-3).

GRECIAN OPPRESSION

During the reign of Cambyses, the son of Cyrus, the work of the Temple and the city ceased (Ezra 4:1-24). During the second year of his own reign Darius I reconfirmed the decree of Cyrus, and the Restoration began again. The Temple was completed in the sixth year of his reign. The city was not restored fully until the twentieth year of the reign of Artaxerxes (Neh. 2:1 through 6:19). After Jerusalem was rebuilt, Alexander the Great defeated the last king of the Medo-Persian Empire (331 B.C.). The Grecian Empire then became the *fifth* world empire to oppress Israel in *"the times of the Gentiles."*

When Alexander the Great died in 323 B.C., the Grecian Empire was divided among his four generals. Cassander took Greece and Macedon; Lysimachus took most of Asia Minor; Ptolemy took Egypt; and, Seleucus took Syria and the eastern part of the empire, including the modern countries of Iraq and Iran. The future Antichrist will arise from this last division of Greece (Dan. 7:17, 24; 8:8-9; 11:40-45). The land of Palestine, where the Jews had been restored, was claimed by both Syria and Egypt, and many wars were fought between these two countries. The Greek kings of Egypt had dominion over Palestine for about 125 years (323-198 B.C.), and the Greek kings of Syria had dominion for 34 years (198-164 B.C.). The capital of the empire of Seleucus was Antioch, named after his father, Antiochus. Antioch later became the missionary headquarters of the early Christians (Acts 11:26).

Antiochus Epiphanes, the eighth king of Syria, sought to Hellenize the Jews by abolishing their religion and by forcing heathen worship upon them. He invaded Jerusalem (168 B.C.), slaughtered 40,000 Jews in three days, desecrated the Temple, offered a swine on the Altar, and caused the sacrifice to cease.

Under the leadership of Mattathias and his five sons, known as the Maccabees, the Jews revolted. Once again Israel gained her independence, which lasted 100 years. The Maccabean family cleansed and rededicated Zerrubbabel's Temple, and national harmony was reestablished.

In 63 B.C. the Roman Empire under Pompey conquered Palestine, destroyed the Temple, and declared Judea a Roman province. The Roman Empire became the *sixth* world empire to oppress Israel in *"the times of the Gentiles."* The Jews remained under Roman bondage during the Ministry of Jesus and the Apostles (Lk. 2:1-2; Acts 25:10-12).

DISPERSION OF THE JEWS

After the Dispersion, the Jews lived in various lands. Although some remained in Palestine, the majority were Babylonian, Syrian, and Egyptian. Because the Temple had been destroyed, synagogues were constructed as places of worship and teaching. In 280 B.C. Greek-speaking Jews in Alexandria, and Egypt, translated the Hebrew Old Testament into the Greek version known as the Septuagint. It was used widely during the days of Christ and the Apostles.

SADDUCEES

Eventually the Maccabean family was split into factions. The *Sadducees* were drawn largely from the rich land-owning class who had secured a dominant position. They were conservative, to the extent of refusing to accept any revelation beyond the five books of Moses. Thus, they rejected belief in immortality, Resurrection, Angels, and demons. As an aristocratic minority, they had little interest in religion and few followers.

PHARISEES

The *Pharisees* were the religious purists. Their supreme concern and delight was to keep the Law, including the traditions, in every exact detail. They considered themselves the model Jews, and kept themselves apart from other men as far as possible. Their *"holier than thou"* attitude makes their name a term of reproach even today. Their arrogance, combined with a dry legalism that put exact ritual observance before love and Mercy, led them into conflict with Jesus (see Mat., Chpt. 23). He did not dispute their orthodoxy, but the proud and unloving way in which they upheld it. The Pharisees were respected highly by other Jews for their life-style.

ESSENES

The *Essenes* regarded themselves as the true people of God, and all others, including Jewish leaders at Jerusalem, as His enemies. They kept to themselves, occupied in the diligent study of the Scriptures, bound by a strict monastic discipline, loving one another and hating all those outside. The discovery of the Dead Sea Scrolls since 1947 revealed that the Essenes produced elaborate Biblical commentaries, applying every phrase of the Old Testament passages to their own situation and expectations. They looked forward to the coming of two Messiahs, of Aaron (priestly) and of Israel (royal), or possibly one Messiah combining both roles. While the Sadducees and the Pharisees tried to make the best of Roman rule, and the Essenes dreamed of the mighty intervention of God to deliver them, many Jews sought Salvation more actively.

ZEALOTS

The *Zealots* were the *"freedom fighters,"* the revolutionaries of the Jewish people. They founded their appeal on the belief that subjection to Rome was treason to God, the True King of Israel. The Zealots eventually sparked off the great rebellion that led to the Roman destruction of Jerusalem in A.D. 70.

SCRIBES

The *Scribes* were the copyists of the Scriptures. They were the authorities of the Law and originated about the time of Ezra. They cooperated with the Great Synagogue, comprised of 120 men, who formed the Old Testament Canon.

DISTINCTION BETWEEN LAW OF GOD AND LAW OF MOSES

Throughout the entire history of Israel, the Law of Moses had been the standard of conduct; hence, the name of this period is the Dispensation of Law. The expressions *"Law of God"* and *"Law of Moses"* are used interchangeably throughout the Bible. Some modern-day religious sects who keep the Sabbath Day as their day of worship have tried to make distinctions between the Ten Commandments, which they call the Law of God, and the dietary laws, feast days, and other ordinances, which they call the Law of Moses. However, this teaching is contrary to the Bible, for no such distinction is stated.

The word *"Law"* is used in the Bible to refer to the Decalogue (Ten Commandments), the Pentateuch (first five Books of the Old Testament), and the whole Word of God (read Ps. 119). The instructions God gave to Israel through Moses on Mount Sinai also are referred to as the Law. The Jews divided the Old Testament into the Law, the Psalms, and the Prophets. Jesus spoke of *"the Law and the Prophets"* (Mat. 7:12).

The Law that God gave to Israel after their deliverance from Egypt was a whole *unit*, yet consisted of various commandments. Most people have the idea that the only law Moses brought down from the mountain was the tables of stone — the Ten Commandments (Ex., Chpt. 20) — but this was not all. God also gave Moses laws concerning the feast days, Holy days, sacrifices, offerings, dietary laws, civil laws, and the pattern of the Tabernacle. There were many commandments given, but they are all part of the Book of the Law (e.g., read Ex., Chpt. 20 through Lev., Chpt. 27).

GIVING OF THE LAW

At Sinai God gave the Law to Moses, and through Moses to the people. The Law actually was given to Moses *three* separate times. The *first* time God gave it *orally* (Ex. 20:1). The response of the Children of Israel to Moses was this:

"You speak with us, and we will hear: but let not God speak with us, lest we die" (Ex. 20:19).

The people feared the awesome display of the Presence of God. It is apparent that at some point Moses wrote these words of the Lord personally in a book (Ex. 24:3-4). The *second* time God *wrote* the Law on two tables of stone with His Own Finger and delivered them to Moses (Ex. 31:18). Moses returned from the top of the mountain, carrying the tables of stone with him, and beheld the Children of Israel in idolatry, dancing around a golden calf:

"It came to pass, as soon as he came near unto the camp, that he saw the calf, and the dancing: and Moses' anger waxed hot, and he cast the tables out of his hands, and brake them beneath the Mount" (Ex. 32:19).

Again Moses climbed the mountain and for the *third* time God gave him the Ten Commandments. The first tables of stone were the Work of

God; but because Moses had broken them, God commanded him to hew out stones like the ones he had destroyed and climb back up the mountain where God once again wrote the Law (Ex. 34:1-4). The second tables of stone were placed inside the Ark of the Covenant (Deut. 10:1-2).

THREE CATEGORIES OF THE LAW

The whole Law as given to Moses easily can be divided into three parts: moral law, civil law, and ceremonial law. The first governed the *individual* life of the people, the second governed the *national* life of the people, and the third governed the *religious* life of the people.

MORAL LAW

The *moral law*, or the Ten Commandments (Ex. 20:1-17), were the foundation for all the laws. They controlled life for the individual, for the Commandments include the words *"thou"* and *"thy"* 45 times.

These commands divided themselves into two sections, perhaps represented by the two stones. The first four reveal the expected relationship between man and God. The other six reveal the expected relationship between man and his neighbor.

Jesus also taught the importance of this vertical and horizontal association:

"You shall love the Lord your God with all your heart, and with all your soul, and with all your mind. This is the First and great Commandment. And the Second is like unto it, You shall love your neighbour as yourself" (Mat. 22:37-39).

Jesus Himself narrowed down all of the hundreds of laws and ordinances given throughout the Old Testament to these two Commandments when He said:

"On these two Commandments hang ALL THE LAW AND THE PROPHETS" (Mat. 22:40).

CIVIL LAW

The *civil law*, or the judgments (Ex. 21:1 through 23:33), related to the nation, and concerned social affairs.

All of the legislation of the United States is based upon these laws: the protection of the innocent, the punishment of criminals, the law of justice and equality, human rights, and property rights. It may be more correct to say that the laws of the United States *were*, at one time, based upon the Mosaic Law.

The erosion of values and the acceptance of abortion-on-demand and easy divorce, the banning of prayer and Bible reading in the public schools, etc., reveal how far America has strayed from the Judeo-Christian ethic that made this country great!

CEREMONIAL LAW

The *ceremonial law*, or the Ordinances (Ex. 24:12 through 31:18), governed the religious life of the Children of Israel, and is given in greater detail in the Book of Leviticus. The Tabernacle was ordained, designed, and occupied by God Himself (Ex. 25:8).

While the body of the Christian is *"the Temple of God"* (I Cor. 3:17) during this present Dispensation of Grace, the Tabernacle (and later the Temple at Jerusalem) was the dwelling place of God during the Dispensation of Law. Every part of the Tabernacle, every measurement, every piece of furniture, every color, and all of the materials, manifested, in type and shadow, the Divine Truths of the Lord and His Church.

When Moses had completed the construction of the Tabernacle, the Glory of the Lord came down and rested on the Mercy Seat, and the pillar of cloud by day and pillar of fire by night rested on the Tabernacle as an outward evidence of an internal Presence, and by it His People continually were led!

LAWS BEFORE THIS DISPENSATION

The Dispensation of Law should not imply that there were no laws on the Earth before this time. Obviously there were laws during the Dispensation of Human Government (Gen. 9:1-7). Even during the Dispensation of Innocence God had given Adam and Eve the *"Law"* that they should not eat of the Tree of the Knowledge of Good and Evil, lest they die (Gen. 2:17). The Dispensation of Law did, however, reveal God's *entire* Law for mankind, for it covered *every* aspect of his life in great detail.

ISRAEL'S ACCEPTANCE OF THE LAW

After the Children of Israel had given their unconditional promise to keep the Law, on three separate occasions (Ex. 19:3-8; 24:3-4; and 24:7), the Covenant was sealed by the sprinkling of blood, which signified their life was forfeited if they refused to obey (Ex. 24:8). The Law was not *forced* upon them by God or by Moses; it was *accepted* freely by all. And throughout the history of Israel, when they obeyed the Law, they prospered; but when they disobeyed the Law, they suffered!

GOD'S PROVISION FOR ISRAEL

God provided for all of the needs of His People. He gave them food when they were hungry (Ex. 16:11-15), and water when they were thirsty (Ex. 17:5-7). God actually fed them manna from Heaven *every day* for a period of 40 years (Ex. 16:35). During this time of wilderness wandering, God kept their clothes from wearing out, and their shoes never wore one single hole (Deut. 29:5). This was a remarkable miracle considering the rocky terrain on which they traveled. In fact, the Bible states, for the entire 40 years of walking, their feet did not even swell (Deut. 8:4; Neh. 9:21). God took away their sicknesses, and there was not *one* feeble person in *all* of their tribes (Ex. 15:26; 23:25; Ps. 105:37; 107:20). There were an estimated three million people (cf. Ex. 12:37-38), who lived in Divine health and prosperity for a period of 40 years! However, when they murmured and disobeyed the Law of God, they forfeited these wonderful Blessings (read also Ps. 78; 105; 107).

PURPOSE OF THE LAW

Because man in all of the other Dispensations had proved incapable, in himself, of obeying God's Will, the Lord purposed to give man His Will, in its entirety, during the Dispensation of Law. The Law revealed the Holiness of God, and His desire to have a Holy people (Lev. 19:2).

God organized the Children of Israel, and intended that they be the leading nation of the Earth. He gave them a visible system of worshiping Him, and a place where His Presence continually could dwell. In essence, God's Purpose during this Dispensation was the same as the Dispensation of Promise, with the addition of the Law.

The question as to why God gave the Law of Moses to Israel was answered by the Apostle Paul:

"Wherefore then serves the Law? It was added because of transgressions, till the Seed should come to whom the Promise was made; and it was ordained by Angels in the hand of a mediator" (Gal. 3:19).

This Scripture reveals the beginning of the Law, the end of the Law, and the purpose of the Law. According to the Apostle Paul, the Law was not given until 430 years after God made His Covenant Promises with Abraham (Gal. 3:17). The Law continued until the *"Seed"* should come, which was the Lord Jesus Christ. The Law was *"added"* to the Promises that God had given to Abraham and his seed, which were the basis of God's dealings with man during the Dispensation of Promise. If man had continued to believe God and take Him at His Word, the Law would have been unnecessary. The Law was *"added because of transgressions"*

(Gal. 3:19); or, in order to reveal sin as a transgression. Before the Law was given, there was no transgression of the Law:

"For where no Law is, there is no transgression" (Rom. 4:15).

Before the Law was given, there was sin and there was rebellion, but it was not by definition a *"transgression"* of the Law, for the Law had not yet been given. Obviously, transgression of the Law is sin; but before the Law came, there was sin, even though it was not defined as a transgression of the Law, because the Law did not yet exist. Sin was just as wicked and horrible before the Law was given as it was after it came. Paul clearly stated:

"For until the Law SIN WAS IN THE WORLD: BUT sin is not imputed (as a transgression) *when there is no Law"* (Rom. 5:13).

When the Law was *"added,"* it gave sin a new meaning, for then sin became a *transgression* of the Law. For example, it is *wrong* for a child to play in the middle of the street, but the child does not become *disobedient* in doing so until he is instructed that it is unsafe and, therefore, wrong. He then *"breaks the rules"* and transgresses against authority.

The Purpose of the Law was to reveal sin as *rebellion* against the Lord, as a *transgression* against His Commandment, as the Scriptures declare:

"Now we know that what things soever the Law says, it says to them who are under the Law: that every mouth may be stopped, and all the world may become guilty before God. Therefore by the deeds of the Law there shall no flesh be justified in His sight: for BY THE LAW IS THE KNOWLEDGE OF SIN" (Rom. 3:19-20).

The Law made the entire human population guilty before God, so that God could have Mercy upon all persons alike.

GOD'S GRACE IN THIS DISPENSATION

It is important to understand that God manifested His *GRACE* many times during the Dispensation of Law and even before this time. Although God deals with us today in the *fullness* of His Grace, He also showed His Love and Mercy to His People prior to the Dispensation of Grace. In fact, Stephen referred to Israel as *"THE CHURCH in the wilderness"*:

"This is he, who was in THE CHURCH in the wilderness with the Angel which spoke to him in the Mount Sina, and with our fathers: who received the lively oracles to give unto us" (Acts 7:38).

The Greek word translated *"church"* in this Passage is *ekklesia* and used also of the New Testament Church. It simply means *"an assembly of called out ones."* Abraham was *"called out"* from among his kindred (Gen. 12:1), so that Israel would be a nation *"called out"* from among the heathen to serve the Living and True God. The New Testament Church, in the same sense, has been *"called out"* from among the sinful world, to be a separate and Holy people before God.

OLD TESTAMENT SAINTS AND
NEW TESTAMENT BLESSINGS

It has been taught erroneously that the Old Testament Saints did not enjoy the Spiritual Blessings now received by the New Testament Church. However, a proper understanding of the Atonement of Christ proves otherwise. The Blood that Jesus shed for man's Redemption flowed *back* to cover the sins of men before Calvary and *forward* to cover the sins of men since Calvary! It was symbolized as far *back* as the skins with which God covered Adam and Eve after the Fall (Gen. 3:21), and *continued* through *each* Dispensation symbolized by the Offerings of Burnt Sacrifice (Gen. 4:4; 8:20; 22:13; Ex. 29:18; etc.).

We appropriate the benefits of Calvary, during the Dispensation of Grace, *by Faith in the finished Work of Christ,* in the same way as the Old Testament Saints claimed them by *Faith in the Promises of the coming Redeemer.* If Christ had not died, neither the Old Testament Saints nor the New Testament Saints would have been redeemed:

"But Christ being come an High Priest of good things to come, by a greater and more perfect Tabernacle, not made with hands, that is to say, not of this building; Neither by the blood of goats and calves, but BY HIS OWN BLOOD He entered in ONCE into the Holy Place, HAVING OBTAINED ETERNAL REDEMPTION FOR US. For if the blood of bulls and of goats, and the ashes of an heifer sprinkling the unclean, Sanctifies to the purifying of the flesh: HOW MUCH MORE SHALL THE BLOOD OF CHRIST, WHO THROUGH THE ETERNAL SPIRIT OFFERED HIMSELF WITHOUT SPOT TO GOD, PURGE YOUR CONSCIENCE FROM DEAD WORKS TO SERVE THE LIVING GOD? And FOR THIS CAUSE HE IS THE MEDIATOR OF THE NEW TESTAMENT, THAT BY MEANS OF DEATH, FOR THE REDEMPTION OF THE TRANSGRESSIONS THAT WERE UNDER THE FIRST TESTAMENT, THEY WHICH ARE CALLED MIGHT RECEIVE THE PROMISE OF ETERNAL INHERITANCE" (Heb. 9:11-15).

It could not be stated more clearly, that the Redemptive Work of Christ purchased the same Blessings of the Old Testament Saints as well as the New Testament Church! The blood of bulls and goats offered before the Cross could not take away sins anymore than it can today. But the obedience of the Old Testament Saints, mixed with their Faith in the coming Redeemer, of which the sacrifice was a Type, *DID* take away their sins

(Heb. 10:10-18). Old Testament Saints received by Faith virtually all of the Spiritual Blessings available to any Child of God who believes:

1. THEY WERE BORN-AGAIN.

"Of the Rock Who BEGAT YOU you are unmindful, and have forgotten God Who formed you" (Deut. 32:18).

"And did all drink the same spiritual drink: for THEY DRANK OF THAT SPIRITUAL ROCK THAT FOLLOWED THEM: AND THAT ROCK WAS CHRIST" (I Cor. 10:4).

"And the Scripture, foreseeing that God would justify the heathen through Faith, PREACHED BEFORE THE GOSPEL UNTO ABRAHAM, saying, In you shall the nations be blessed" (Gal. 3:8).

"For I am not ashamed of the GOSPEL of Christ: for IT IS THE POWER OF GOD UNTO SALVATION TO EVERY ONE WHO BELIEVES; to the JEW FIRST, and also to the Greek" (Rom. 1:16).

Many other Scriptures teach that the Old Testament Saints received all of the benefits of the New Birth, including Forgiveness, Justification, and Sanctification (Ex. 31:13; Lev. 4:26; Ps. 19:7; 34:22; 51:2; Isa. 45:25; Rom. 4:1-8; Gal. 3:6-14; *et al*).

2. THEY RECEIVED DIVINE HEALING.

"So Abraham prayed unto God: and GOD HEALED ABIMELECH, AND HIS WIFE, AND HIS MAIDSERVANTS; AND THEY BORE CHILDREN" (Gen. 20:17).

"FOR I AM THE LORD WHO HEALS YOU" (Ex. 15:26).

"Bless the Lord, O my soul, and forget not all His benefits: Who forgives all your iniquities; WHO HEALS ALL YOUR DISEASES" (Ps. 103:2-3).

"HE SENT HIS WORD, AND HEALED THEM, AND DELIVERED THEM FROM THEIR DESTRUCTIONS" (Ps. 107:20).

Many other individuals received healing through obedience and prayer (Num. 12:13; 21:9; I Ki. 17:17-24; II Ki. 5:14; *et al*).

3. THEY EXPERIENCED THE POWER OF THE HOLY SPIRIT.

"And I HAVE FILLED HIM WITH THE SPIRIT OF GOD, in wisdom, and in understanding, and in knowledge, and in all manner of workmanship" (Ex. 31:3).

"But truly I AM FULL OF POWER BY THE SPIRIT OF THE LORD" (Mic. 3:8).

"And Pharaoh said unto his servants, Can we find such a one as this is, A MAN IN WHOM THE SPIRIT OF GOD IS?" (Gen. 41:38).

"Then Samuel took the horn of oil, and anointed him in the midst of his brethren: AND THE SPIRIT OF THE LORD CAME UPON DAVID FROM THAT DAY FORWARD" (I Sam. 16:13).

Many received various measures of the Holy Spirit, although none were baptized in the Holy Spirit until after Pentecost (Judg. 3:10; II Ki. 2:9; Dan. 4:18; Jn. 7:37-39; *et al*).

4. THEY HAD THE FRUIT OF THE SPIRIT.
    Love (Deut. 6:5; II Sam. 1:26; *et al*);
    Joy (I Chron. 12:40; Ezra 3:13; Job 33:26; *et al*);
    Peace (Num. 6:26; Ps. 4:8; Isa. 26:3; *et al*);
    Longsuffering (Ps. 40:1; Eccl. 7:8; *et al*);
    Gentleness (II Sam. 18:5; 22:36; *et al*);
    Goodness (II Chron. 32:32; Ps. 107:9; *et al*);
    Faith (Hab. 2:4; Neh. 7:2; Heb. 11:1-40; *et al*);
    Meekness (Num. 12:3; Ps. 22:26; 25:9; *et al*); *and,*
    Temperance (I Ki. 22:6; Jer. 20:9; *et al*).

5. THEY HAD THE GIFTS OF THE SPIRIT.
    Word of Wisdom (Ex. 28:3; 36:1; II Sam. 14:20; *et al*);
    Word of Knowledge (Jer. 11:18; Dan. 1:17; *et al*);
    Faith (Rom. 4:1-25; Heb. 11:1-40; *et al*);
    Healings (Gen. 20:17; Num. 12:13; *et al*);
    Miracles (Ex. 14:21-22; II Ki. 6:5-7; *et al*);
    Prophecy (Num. 11:25; I Sam. 10:10; *et al*); and,
    Discerning of spirits (I Ki. 3:16-27; II Ki. 5:25-27; *et al*).

The only Gifts of the Spirit not manifested by Old Testament Saints were Tongues and Interpretation of Tongues, which were not given until after Pentecost (Acts 2:4). However, there were interpretations of dreams, visions, etc. (Dan. 1:17; 5:25-28; *et al*).

God demonstrated His Grace in a marvelous way under the Dispensation of the Law. Many of the Old Testament Saints far exceeded modern Believers in yielding to God and being used by the Spirit. Because we live during the Dispensation of Grace, which is a *"better Covenant . . . established upon better Promises"* (Heb. 8:6), we stand without excuse if we are not believing God for His miraculous Power in the Church today.

LAW AND CHURCH

God never intended for the Law to be binding upon the New Testament Church. The Law *"was added . . . TILL the Seed should come"* (Gal. 3:19). After Jesus came to *"fulfill"* the Law (Mat. 5:17-18), it no longer was needed:

"Moreover the LAW entered, that the offence might abound. But where sin abounded, GRACE did much more abound" (Rom. 5:20).

"For the LAW was given by MOSES, but GRACE and Truth came by JESUS CHRIST" (Jn. 1:17).

"For CHRIST IS THE END OF THE LAW for Righteousness to everyone who believes" (Rom. 10:4).

"He takes away the FIRST (Covenant), *that He may establish the SECOND* (Covenant)*"* (Heb. 10:9).

"Wherefore the Law was our schoolmaster to bring us unto Christ, that we might be justified by Faith. But after that Faith is come, WE ARE NO LONGER UNDER A SCHOOLMASTER" (Gal. 3:24-25).

While Christ ministered here on Earth, He perfectly *fulfilled* every part of the Law. God sent His Son into the world to do for man what the Law had been unable to do:

"For what the Law could NOT do, in that it was weak through the flesh, God sending His Own Son in the likeness of sinful flesh, and for sin, condemned sin in the flesh: That the Righteousness of the Law might be fulfilled in us, who walk not after the flesh, but after the Spirit" (Rom. 8:3-4).

After Christ completed His Mission, the Law was abolished *completely*:

"For He is our peace, Who has made both one, and has broken down the middle wall of partition between us; HAVING ABOLISHED IN HIS FLESH, the enmity, EVEN THE LAW OF COMMANDMENTS CONTAINED IN ORDINANCES; for to make in Himself of twain one new man, so making peace" (Eph. 2:14-15).

When Christ cried from the Cross, *"It is finished"* (Jn. 19:30), He meant exactly what He said! The Law had served its purpose, and was *completed*. His statement, *It is finished,"* also had reference to the following:

1. THE OLD TESTAMENT PROPHECIES CONCERNING HIS LIFE AND ATONING DEATH (Ps. 22; Isa. 53; etc.);

2. THE DEFEAT OF SATAN (Jn. 12:31-32; Col. 2:14-17; Heb. 2:14-15);

3. THE CANCELLATION OF THE POWER OF SIN (Rom. 6:1-23; I Cor. 15:54-58);

4. THE PLAN OF SALVATION FROM SIN (Mat. 26:28; Eph. 1:7; Col. 1:14; Heb. 9:15);

5. BODILY HEALING FOR EVERY BELIEVER (Isa. 53:4-5; Mat. 8:17; James 5:14-16; I Pet. 2:24); and,

6. THE WAY OF PERSONAL ACCESS TO GOD FOR EVERY BELIEVER (Mat. 27:51; Eph. 2:14-18; Heb. 10:19-22).

Second Corinthians 3:6-18 teaches that the Old Covenant, which was the Law of Moses, was *"done away,"* and *"abolished,"* at Calvary and that the New Covenant has taken its place. This Passage also states that the *"ministration of death, written and engraved in stones,"* or the Ten Commandments, was abolished. New Testament Christians are not obligated to keep the Ten Commandments as revealed in the Old Covenant.

We are *now* responsible to keep only those Commandments that were made a part of the New Covenant.

All of the Ten Commandments can be found in the New Covenant with the exception of the Fourth Commandment, *"Remember the Sabbath day, to keep it Holy"* (Ex. 20:8). The Apostle Paul made it clear that we are not bound to keep the Jewish Sabbath, Saturday, as our day of worship, since Christ abolished the Law on the Cross:

"Blotting out the handwriting of Ordinances that was against us, which was contrary to us, and took it out of the way, nailing it to His Cross . . . LET NO MAN THEREFORE JUDGE YOU IN MEAT, OR IN DRINK, OR IN RESPECT OF AN HOLYDAY, OR OF THE NEW MOON, OR OF THE SABBATH DAYS" (Col. 2:14-16).

All of the New Testament teaching regarding the Sabbath Day, or Seventh Day, observance proves unmistakably that this day of worship belonged to Israel under the Law and that in Christ it has been done away!

SABBATH AND CHURCH

The Apostle Paul plainly taught that under the New Covenant man is not *bound* to keep *any one* particular day as the Sabbath:

"One man esteems one day above another: another esteems every day alike. Let every man be fully persuaded in his own mind. He that regards the day, regards it unto the Lord; and he who regards not the day, to the Lord he does not regard it" (Rom. 14:5-6).

However, it is clear from Scripture and history that the early Christians established the tradition of meeting for worship on the first day of the week, *Sunday,* which they called the Lord's Day. The Romans set aside certain days to worship the emperor and called them Augustean Day, Nero's Day, etc. Therefore, Christians set aside Sunday as their day to worship God and called it the Lord's Day, as mentioned by John the Revelator:

"I was in the Spirit on the LORD'S DAY" (Rev. 1:10).

There are various reasons why the early Christians chose Sunday as their day of worship. It was a celebration of the Resurrection of Christ which occurred on the first day of the week (Mat. 28:1-7; Mk. 16:1-7; Lk. 24:1-7; Jn. 20:1-9). Following His Resurrection, Christ appeared to the Disciples two separate times on the first day of the week (Jn. 20:19, 26). God chose to pour out His Spirit on the Day of Pentecost, which occurred on Sunday (Acts 2:1-4). Concerning this, Irenaeus, one of the Early Church fathers, wrote in A.D. 178:

"The mystery of the Lord's Resurrection may not be celebrated on any other day than the Lord's Day . . . Pentecost fell on the first day of

the week, and was therefore associated with the Lord's Day."

It was on the first day of the week that God gave the Apostle John the Book of Revelation (Rev. 1:10). There are other Scriptures that clearly teach that the early Christians met together on Sunday to worship the Lord:

"And upon the FIRST DAY OF THE WEEK, when the Disciples came together to break bread, Paul preached unto them, ready to depart on the morrow; and continued his speech until midnight" (Acts 20:7).

"Upon the FIRST DAY OF THE WEEK let every one of you lay by him in store, as God has prospered him, that there be no gatherings when I come" (I Cor. 16:2).

No example is found in history and no apostolic command is given in Scripture that Christians should gather for worship on the seventh day, the old Jewish Sabbath. A careful study of the matter reveals a striking contrast between the Jewish Sabbath and the Christian Lord's Day.

• The Sabbath was the seventh day of the week; the Lord's Day is the first day of the week.

• During the Dispensation of Law compulsory obedience of the Sabbath was demanded; during the Dispensation of Grace voluntary worship and service is expected on the Lord's Day.

• The Sabbath was part of the Old Covenant; the Lord's Day is part of the New Covenant.

• The Sabbath was given to *Israel* under the Law; the Lord's Day is given to the *Christian* under Grace.

• The Sabbath was a day of *rest* for the Jew; the Lord's Day is a day of *worship* for the Christian.

Those who adhere to the seventh day as their day of worship do not *fully* observe the Sabbath as God commanded. The Law limited travel on the Sabbath to 2,000 cubits, about two-thirds of a mile (Act 1:12)! Cooking (Ex. 16:23), working (Ex. 20:8-10), gathering wood (Num. 15:32-36), and kindling a fire (Ex. 35:2-3), all were forbidden on the Sabbath under the penalty of death (Ex. 31:13-15).

The Scriptures teach that Sabbaths are to be observed in the Millennium and the New Earth, so that all flesh can come before God to worship (Isa. 66:22-24; Ezek. 44:24; 45:17; 46:3). However, the word *"Sabbath"* simply means *"rest or cessation from labor"* and may denote a time span of *one day* (Ex. 20:8-11), *one year* (Lev. 25), or an *eternity* (Heb. 4:9). No Scripture reveals which particular day will be observed as the Sabbath during this future time, but it is certain that keeping the seventh day as the Sabbath is not binding upon the Christian during the Dispensation of Grace.

LAW AND GRACE

There are also contrasts between the Law of Moses during the Dispensation of Law and the Grace of God during the Dispensation of Grace.

• The Law *demanded* Holiness, but Grace *gives* Holiness.

• Under the Law the *sheep* died for the shepherd, but under Grace the *Shepherd* died for the sheep.

• The Law *condemned* the best man, but Grace *saves* the worst sinner.

• The Law of Moses *revealed* man's sin, but the Grace of God *covers* man's sin.

• The Law of Moses *cursed* the sinner, but the Grace of God *blesses* the Believer.

• The Law placed man under *bondage*, but Grace sets the prisoner *free!*

FAILURE OF MAN

It goes without saying that man failed God under the Dispensation of Law as he had in every preceding Dispensation. Because man failed, God sent His Judgment. The Nation of Israel was judged because of their long rebellion against God, which culminated in their rejection and Crucifixion of the Messiah God had sent to liberate them. In A.D. 70 Jerusalem once again was destroyed by the armies of General Titus, and one million people were killed. Israel has continued to suffer Judgment and oppression down through the centuries. The words that the Jews shouted at the trial of Christ before Pilate, have become, sadly a Prophecy fulfilled:

"Then answered all the people, and said, HIS BLOOD BE ON US, AND ON OUR CHILDREN" (Mat. 27:25).

The Judgment of the whole world of every age was borne by Jesus Christ at Calvary. He suffered for our sins, so that we could go free! He died as our substitute! His stripes purchased our healing! The Sacrifice of Christ on the Cross — PAID IT ALL!

> *"Oh, the love that drew Salvation's Plan!*
> *"Oh, the Grace that brought it down to man!*
> *"Oh, the mighty gulf that God did span*
> *"At Calvary!"*

> *"Mercy there was great, and Grace was free;*
> *"Pardon there was multiplied to me;*
> *"There my burdened soul found liberty,*
> *"At Calvary!"*

We shall discuss further this wonderful truth in the next Chapter.

Chapter 10

The Dispensation Of Grace

Continued . . .

CHAPTER TEN

THE DISPENSATION OF GRACE

THE OLD TESTAMENT REVEALED IN
THE NEW TESTAMENT

It has been stated that the Old Testament is the New Testament *concealed*, and the New Testament is the Old Testament *revealed*. The Law prepared the way for the promised Messiah, the Lord Jesus Christ:

"Wherefore the Law was our schoolmaster TO BRING US UNTO CHRIST, that we might be justified by Faith" (Gal. 3:24).

Each of the past Dispensations manifested two things: (1) the ever-increasing evidence of the sin and guilt of fallen man and (2) the ever-unfolding Plan of God to send a Redeemer into the world. God first showed through the animal sacrifices that *"it is the Blood that maketh an Atonement for the soul"* (Lev. 17:11). Every sacrifice was an execution of the sentence of the Law upon a substitute for the sinner. Through the offerings of the people, God was pointing sinners to the Savior who was yet to come. As time passed, God continued to reveal His Plan ever so subtly to the searching heart.

PROMISE OF A REDEEMER

At the close of the Dispensation of Innocence, God announced that the Redeemer would be the *"Seed"* of the woman (Gen. 3:15).

In the Dispensation of Conscience, God continued the revelation by accepting Abel's *blood* sacrifice and by refusing Cain's offering (Gen. 4:4-5).

In the Dispensation of Human Government, a blessing was pronounced upon Shem, through whom the *"Seed"* should come (Gen. 9:26).

In the Dispensation of Promise, it was revealed that the Redeemer would come from the Nation of Israel and from the Tribe of Judah (Gen. 12:3; 49:10).

During the Dispensation of Law, God promised David that his family would bring forth the Savior (II Sam 7:12-16).

Then, 700 years before Jesus came into the world, Micah the Prophet named the very place where He was to be born (Mic. 5:2).

God revealed to Isaiah that Christ was to be born of a virgin (Isa. 7:14) and further stated:

"For unto us a Child is born, unto us a Son is given: and the Government shall be upon His Shoulder: and His Name shall be called

Wonderful, Counsellor, The Mighty God, The Everlasting Father, The Prince of Peace" (Isa. 9:6).

The Lord revealed to Daniel the very time of His Coming into the world — 600 years before Christ was born in Bethlehem (Dan. 9:24-26).

REDEEMER'S DEATH FORETOLD

Old Testament writers foretold in minute detail the sufferings of Christ and the manner of His Death:

• He was to be betrayed by a friend (Ps. 41:9; Mat. 26:49-50);

• He was to be sold for 30 pieces of silver (Zech. 11:12; Mat. 26:15);

• He was to be forsaken by His Disciples (Zech. 13:7; Mat. 26:31; Mk. 14:27);

• He was to be accused by false witnesses (Ps. 35:11; Mat. 26:59-60);

• He was to be spat upon and beaten with many stripes (Isa. 50:6; 53:5; Mat. 27:26; Mk. 14:65);

• He was to be nailed to a Cross (Ps. 22:16; Mat. 27:35; Lk. 23:33);

• He was to be mocked while hanging on the Cross (Ps. 22:7-8; Mat. 27:39-40);

• He was to be pierced with a sword (Zech. 12:10; Jn. 19:33-37);

• He was to be offered vinegar and gall to drink (Ps. 69:21; Mat. 27:34);

• None of His Bones were to be broken (Ps. 34:20; Jn. 19:33-37);

• He was to be crucified with thieves (Isa. 53:9-12; Mat. 27:38; Mk. 15:27-28);

• Soldiers were to gamble for His garments (Ps. 22:18; Mat. 27:35); and,

• He was to be buried as a rich man (Isa. 53:9; Mat. 27:57-60).

REDEEMER'S SECOND ADVENT FORETOLD

The Old Testament Prophets not only foretold the First Advent of Christ as a *suffering Savior*, but also prophesied of His Second Advent as a *Glorious King.*

Isaiah foretold that the Government would be upon His Shoulders and that He would reign upon the throne of David (Isa. 9:6-7).

Jeremiah stated that He was to be a Righteous King who would have a prosperous reign and execute Judgment upon the Earth, delivering Israel from her enemies (Jer. 23:5-6).

Daniel prophesied that Christ would return and set up an everlasting Kingdom (Dan. 7:13-14).

Many other Scriptures contain Prophecies of the coming of Messiah (Isa. 32:1-4, 15-20; Zech. 14:4-9, etc.).

SEPARATION OF FIRST ADVENT AND
SECOND ADVENT BY THIS DISPENSATION

The ironic element of these Old Testament Prophecies is that the Prophets did not perceive the time span between the First Advent of Christ as Redeemer and the Second Advent of Christ as King of kings! The Apostle Peter clearly detected this:

"Of which Salvation the Prophets have enquired and searched diligently, who Prophesied of the Grace that should come unto you: Searching what, or WHAT MANNER OF TIME the Spirit of Christ which was in them DID SIGNIFY, when it testified beforehand the SUFFERINGS of Christ, and the GLORY that should follow" (I Pet. 1:10-11).

The religious leaders of Jesus' day did not separate the many Prophecies that foretold His *Sufferings* from the Prophecies that foretold His *Glory*; therefore, they rejected Christ as their Messiah. They believed that all of the Prophecies that referred to the Messiah were to be fulfilled at His First Coming. They failed to see that the *Cross* of Christ would precede His *Crown*. This span of time they failed to discern: separating the First Advent and the Second Advent of Christ is the *Dispensation of Grace*, the period in which we presently live.

The Prophecies of the Old Testament may be compared to the separate peaks of one mountain. When viewed from a distance, the peaks appear to be close, almost touching. But the nearer a person gets to the mountain, the peaks are seen to be many miles apart, separated by deep valleys. The Old Testament Prophet failed to see the *"valley"* of the *Church Age* that separated the First Coming and Second Coming of Jesus Christ. The Prophet Isaiah stated that the Messiah would come *". . . to proclaim the acceptable year of the LORD, and the day of vengeance of our God"* (Isa. 61:2).

These two events, which he separated with a mere comma, actually span a period covering the entire Dispensation of Grace, which already has lasted nearly 2,000 years! Likewise Jeremiah made no distinction between the coming of *"a Righteous Branch"* and the coming of *"a King* (that) *shall reign"* (Jer. 23:5-6). Other examples of this great parenthesis separating the two Advents of Christ are Palms 2:6-7; Isaiah 9:6-7; 11:1-5; Daniel 9:25-27; Micah 5:1-4; etc. As the Prophecies concerning Christ's First Advent were *literally* fulfilled, so also will be the many Prophecies concerning His Second Coming!

FULNESS OF GOD'S GRACE

The Dispensation in which we now are living is referred to as the Dispensation of Grace, because of the *fulness* of the *Grace of God* being manifested to us through the Life, Death, and Resurrection of Jesus Christ:

"For the Law was given by Moses, but GRACE and Truth came by Jesus Christ" (Jn. 1:17).

Even as there were laws for mankind *before* the Dispensation of Law, God's Grace was in operation *before* the Dispensation of Grace.

It was Grace, at the end of the Dispensation of Innocence that clothed Adam and Eve with animal skins as a Type of the coming Redeemer (Gen. 3:21).

It was Grace that dealt with man in the Dispensation of Conscience before the Flood, for *"Noah found GRACE in the sight of the Lord"* (Gen. 6:8).

It was Grace, during the Dispensation of Law — when Moses lifted up the serpent in the wilderness, as a Type of Christ being lifted up on the Cross — that brought Salvation and healing to the people (Num. 21:5-9; Jn. 3:14).

Although God showed mankind His Grace in various episodes, it was not until the Dispensation of Grace that God poured out His Grace without measure in its entirety, through the Lord Jesus Christ.

DEFINITION OF DISPENSATION OF GRACE

The definition of *"Grace"* has been stated popularly as *"unmerited favor."* The Greek word translated *"Grace"* is *charis,* from which we derive the word *"charismatic." "Grace"* simply means *"favor, gift, or benefit."* As applied to the Grace of God, it is that which God gives to man totally apart from his worthiness or unworthiness.

What God bestows as a gift cannot be earned, nor can it be repaid. All of the Blessings of God come to us through His marvelous Grace! We deserve nothing, but He gives us everything! If we could *earn* the Blessings of God, they would no longer be *gifts,* but *rewards.* The Gifts of God such as Salvation, the Baptism with the Holy Spirit, Divine healing, etc., are given to man purely through God's Grace (Eph. 2:8-9; Acts 11:15-17; James 5:15).

The service that we render for God's Kingdom, *after* He saves us by His Grace, will be rewarded at the Judgment Seat of Christ (I Cor. 3:11-15; Rom. 14:10). But this does not mean that we are *earning* our Salvation or any other gift from God, for they are imparted by His Sovereign

Grace, through the *Faith* of the Believer. The Grace of God in this Dispensation is illustrated beautifully by the words of the Apostle Paul:

"He Who spared not His Own Son, but delivered Him up for us all, how shall He not with Him also FREELY give us ALL things?" (Rom. 8:32).

If a person is under Law, he is not under Grace; and if he is under Grace, he is not under Law:

"For sin shall not have dominion over you: FOR YOU ARE NOT UNDER THE LAW, BUT UNDER GRACE" (Rom. 6:14).

A person is *"under the Law"* when he tries to gain the Blessings of God by the performance of good works and the observance of ceremonies. A person is *"under Grace"* when he gains the Blessings of God by trusting in God's Work for him and not in his work for God.

It is deep-rooted in the heart of mankind to strive in order to *save himself.* This is a total impossibility!

CONTRAST BETWEEN OLD COVENANT AND NEW COVENANT

The Dispensation of Grace, or the New Covenant, replaced the Dispensation of Law, or the Old Covenant (Mat. 26:28; Heb. 8:13). The reason for which the Old Covenant was done away is stated:

"Who also has made us able Ministers of THE NEW TESTAMENT; not of the letter, but of the Spirit: FOR THE LETTER KILLS, BUT THE SPIRIT GIVES LIFE" (II Cor. 3:6).

When Jesus Christ established the New Covenant, He came to give *life* more abundantly (Jn. 10:10). (The following chart is a contrast between the Old Covenant and the New Covenant.)

Jesus Christ took away the Old Covenant that He might establish the New Covenant (Heb. 10:9). He did this by fulfilling the Law (Mat. 5:18) through His Life, abolishing it (Eph. 2:15) through His Death, and nailing it to His Cross (Col. 2:14). Since that time the New Covenant has been in effect.

OLD COVENANT	NEW COVENANT
1. Given by Moses (Jn. 1:17)	1. Given by Jesus Christ (Mat. 26:28)
2. Law of Moses (Acts 13:39)	2. Law of Christ (Gal. 6:2)

OLD COVENANT	NEW COVENANT
3. Law of the flesh (Rom. 8:3)	3. Law of the Spirit (Rom. 8:2)
4. Not of Faith (Gal. 3:12)	4. Law of Faith (Rom. 3:27)
5. Yoke of bondage (Gal. 5:1)	5. Law of Liberty (James 1:25)
6. Ended with Christ (Rom. 10:4)	6. Began with Christ (Mk. 14:24)
7. Brought death (II Cor. 3:7)	7. Brought life (Heb. 10:19-20)
8. Declared man guilty (Rom. 3:19)	8. Declared man not guilty (Acts 13:39)
9. Abolished (Eph. 2:15)	9. Still in force (Heb. 10:9)
10. Demanded Righteousness (Gal. 3:10)	10. Gave Righteousness (Gal. 5:18-23)
11. Could not save from sin (Heb. 10:4)	11. Saves to the uttermost (Heb. 7:25)
12. Had many sacrifices (Heb. 10:1)	12. Had only One Sacrifice (Heb. 10:10-14)
13. Remembered sins (Heb. 10:3)	13. Forgets sins (Heb. 8:12)
14. Law of works (Gal. 3:10)	14. Law of Grace (Eph. 2:8-9)
15. Brought wrath (Rom. 4:15)	15. Delivered from wrath (Rom. 5:9)

LENGTH OF THIS DISPENSATION

The length of the Dispensation of Grace is figured from the First Advent of Christ to His Second Advent. It already has lasted nearly 2,000 years! How long it will continue is known only to God (Mat. 24:36). The Dispensation of Grace has lasted much longer than any previous Dispensation, showing the Grace and Mercy of God extended toward mankind! It is God's Will that the entire world hear the Gospel Message before the end of this Age:

"One day is with the Lord as a thousand years, and a thousand years as one day. The Lord is not slack concerning His Promise, as some men count slackness; but is longsuffering to us-ward, not willing that any should perish, but that all should come to Repentance. But the Day of the Lord will come" (II Pet. 3:8-10).

"THIS GOSPEL of the Kingdom shall be preached in all the world for a witness unto all nations; and then shall the end come" (Mat. 24:14).

If the Rapture of the Church were to occur as you read this sentence, there still would be at least seven years left in this Dispensation, for the Antichrist will be in power for seven years after he is revealed (Dan. 9:27). He cannot be revealed until *after* the Rapture of the Church (II Thess. 2:7-8), and until *after* the formation of the ten nations inside the territory of the Old Roman Empire (Dan. 7:24).

DIVINE METHOD OF REDEMPTION

God's method of Redemption was the *"Seed"* of the woman (Gen. 3:15). The One who fulfilled all of the Prophecies concerning the coming Redeemer was the Second Person of the Godhead, the Lord Jesus Christ. In the Incarnation, Christ became the Son of God, being born of the virgin Mary (Lk. 2:1-20). It was necessary that He be both human and Divine so that He might be the Mediator between man and God:

"There is one God, and one Mediator between God and men, THE MAN Christ Jesus" (I Tim. 2:5).

Only through God being made flesh could reconciliation between a Holy God and sinful mankind take place. This was realized in Jesus Christ as *Immanuel* (Mat. 1:23) — GOD WITH US:

"All things are of God, Who has reconciled us to Himself BY JESUS CHRIST, and has given to us the Ministry of Reconciliation; To wit, that GOD WAS IN CHRIST, RECONCILING THE WORLD UNTO HIM-SELF, not imputing their trespasses unto them; and has committed unto us the Word of Reconciliation" (II Cor. 5:18-19).

As man Jesus associated with us in temptation, suffering, and death, yet *"without sin."*

"For we have not an High Priest which cannot be touched with the feeling of our infirmities; BUT WAS IN ALL POINTS TEMPTED LIKE AS WE ARE, YET WITHOUT SIN" (Heb. 4:15).

"And the WORD was made FLESH, and dwelt among US" (Jn. 1:14).

"Christ also suffered for us, leaving us an example, that we should follow His steps: WHO DID NO SIN, NEITHER WAS GUILE FOUND IN HIS MOUTH: Who, when He was reviled, reviled not again; when He suffered, He threatened not; but committed Himself to Him Who judges Righteously: Who His Own Self bare our sins in His Own Body on the tree, that we, being dead to sins, should live unto Righteousness" (I Pet. 2:21-24).

KENOSIS OF CHRIST

The life that Christ lived in the flesh was described by the Apostle Paul:

"Let this mind be in you, which was also in Christ Jesus: Who, being in the form of God, thought it not robbery to be equal with God: BUT MADE HIMSELF OF NO REPUTATION, AND TOOK UPON HIM THE FORM OF A SERVANT, AND WAS MADE IN THE LIKENESS OF MEN: And being found in fashion as a man, He humbled Himself, and became obedient unto death, even the death of the Cross" (Phil. 2:5-8).

Prior to the Incarnation, Christ was co-eternal and co-equal with God the Father and God the Holy Spirit:

"In the beginning was the Word, and the Word was with God, AND THE WORD WAS GOD" (Jn. 1:1).

The *kenosis* of Christ referred to in Philippians 2:7 is taken from the phrase *"made Himself of no reputation,"* and speaks of Christ, literally, *"emptying Himself."* In taking human form Christ divested Himself of the power to use His Divine *Attributes*, laid aside His Glory which He had with the Father eternally, and became limited in knowledge, wisdom, power, glory, and in every other way that man is limited. He DID NOT lay aside His DEITY or His DIVINE NATURE, for then He would have ceased to be God! Because Christ was born of a woman, without a human father, He was human, yet *did not* possess the *fallen human nature* that came through Adam (Rom. 5:12). So Jesus Christ was indeed *FULLY GOD* and yet *FULLY MAN*.

This explains how Christ as God, and yet man, could be tempted (Lk. 4:1-13), and could in all other ways relate to the people He came to save. He did no miracle until He received the fullness of the Spirit (Jn. 1:33; 2:11), and the same power that He possessed is promised to every Believer (Mk. 16:17-18; Lk. 24:49; Jn. 7:37-39; 14:16-18, 26; 16:7-14; Acts 1:8; 2:4, 38-39; etc.). Concerning the miracles He performed, Jesus promised:

"Verily, verily, I say unto you, HE WHO BELIEVES on me, THE WORKS THAT I DO SHALL HE DO ALSO; and GREATER WORKS THAN THESE SHALL HE DO; because I go unto My Father" (Jn. 14:12).

When Christ returned to the Father, He sent the Holy Spirit in all His fullness to empower the Church to carry out the Great Commission (Mat. 28:18-20; Acts 2:33).

DECLARATION OF THE KINGDOM OF GOD

It is revealed in the Scriptures that God has desired to set up a visible kingdom on Earth since the Creation of man, to whom He gave dominion (Gen. 1:26-28). Because man fell, Satan regained dominion and set himself up as *"the prince of this world"* (Mat. 4:8-10; Jn. 14:30).

When God called Abraham, He once again sought to set up a theocratic kingdom on the Earth ruling and reigning through Moses, Joshua, the Elders, the Judges, David, Solomon, the Kings of Israel and Judah down to the Babylonian Captivity. Because the people revolted against God's Plan, and desired a king, the Lord gave them Saul (I Sam. 8:6-7). After Saul failed, God chose David to be king, but because of the failures of his successors, and the idolatry of the people, God's Plan for an earthly kingdom once again was postponed.

God once again attempted to set up His Kingdom on the Earth by sending His Own Son. John the Baptist, as Christ's forerunner, announced that the Kingdom was *"at hand"* (Mat. 3:1-2). When Jesus manifested Himself to Israel, he made the same announcement (Mat. 4:17-23) and commissioned the Twelve (Mat. 10:7) and the Seventy to proclaim the same thing (Lk. 10:1-9). Every time Christ preached the Gospel, healed the sick, and delivered the oppressed, it was a foretaste of the Kingdom Age! The main subjects of the Four Gospels are these:

1.   DECLARATION OF THE KINGDOM (Mat. 4:12 through 7:29; Mk. 1:14-20; Lk. 4:14 through 5:11; Jn. 1:35 through 4:54);

2.   DECLARATION OF THE KING (Mat. 8:1 through 16:20; Mk. 1:21 through 8:30; Lk. 5:12 through 9:21; Jn. 5:1 through 6:71);

3.   REJECTION OF THE KING (Mat. 16:21 through 20:34; Mk. 8:31 through 10:52; Lk. 9:22 through 18:43; Jn. 7:1 through 11:53); and,

4.   REJECTION OF THE KINGDOM (Mat. 21:1 through 26:35;

Mk. 11:1 through 14:25; Lk. 19:1 through 22:38; Jn. 11:54 through 17:26).

The Jews rejected not only the kingdom, but the declaration of it as well (Mat. 22:2-7; Acts 1:6-7; 3:19-26). The earthly kingdom now is postponed until the Second Advent of Jesus Christ (Zech. 14:4-21; Isa. 9:6-7; 11:3-16; Rev. 19:11 through 20:10). Until then Satan continues as ruler of this present world system (II Cor. 4:4).

CONTRAST BETWEEN KINGDOM OF HEAVEN AND KINGDOM OF GOD

The Scriptures teach a distinction between the Kingdom of Heaven and the Kingdom of God. The Kingdom of God is the Reign of God in the Universe over all of His created beings, and includes time and eternity, Heaven and Earth. It is spiritual and *"comes not with observation"* (Lk. 17:20-21). It can be entered only by being *"born again"* (Jn. 3:5-8).

"The KINGDOM OF GOD is not meat and drink; but Righteousness, and Peace, and Joy in the Holy Spirit" (Rom. 14:17).

The Kingdom of Heaven is spoken of only in the Gospel of Matthew where it is mentioned 32 times. Its characteristics are described in the Twelve Parables recorded in Matthew 13:1-50; 18:23-35; 20:1-16; 22:1-14; 25:1-30. The Kingdom of Heaven was the Kingdom of God, and includes everyone who professes to be a part of Christendom. In the Kingdom of Heaven, there is a mixture of good and evil, wheat and tares, wise virgins and foolish virgins.

In the Millennium, the Kingdom of Heaven will become a literal kingdom on the Earth, as God intended. After all of the rebels have been purged from the Kingdom of Heaven (I Cor. 15:24-28), it will be consumed by the Kingdom of God.

Below are some further distinctions between the Kingdom of Heaven and the Kingdom of God:

KINGDOM OF HEAVEN	KINGDOM OF GOD
1. It has a beginning (Lk. 1:32-35).	1. It has no beginning or ending (Lk. 17:20).
2. It is dispensational (I Cor. 15:24-28).	2. It is eternal (Rev. 11:15).
3. It is exclusive (Rev. 5:10).	3. It is all-inclusive (Col. 1:16).

KINGDOM OF HEAVEN	KINGDOM OF GOD
4. It is political (Isa. 9:7).	4. It is spiritual (Rom. 14:17).
5. It is national (Lk. 1:32-33).	5. It is universal (Ps. 103:19).
6. It includes all who profess Christ (Mat. 13:24-30).	6. It includes all who truly *know* Him (Jn. 3:3-5).
7. Men are never told to seek the Kingdom of Heaven.	7. Men are to seek the Kingdom of God (Mat. 6:33).

ANOINTED MINISTRY OF CHRIST

The earthly Ministry of Jesus Christ was foretold by Isaiah the Prophet, for in the synagogue Christ applied these words to Himself:

"The Spirit of the Lord is upon Me, because He has ANOINTED Me TO PREACH the Gospel to the poor; He has sent Me TO HEAL the brokenhearted, TO PREACH deliverance to the captives, and recovering of sight to the blind, TO SET AT LIBERTY them who are bruised, TO PREACH the acceptable Year of the Lord" (Lk. 4:18-19).

It should be noted that the Ministry of Jesus Christ was primarily that of *preaching* (Mat. 4:17; 9:35; Mk. 1:38; 2:2; Lk. 4:43-44; 8:1; 20:1; etc.) and *healing* (Mat. 4:24; 8:7-16; 12:15-22; 14:14; Mk. 5:21-36; Lk. 4:40; 9:11; Jn. 4:46-53). The *Anointing* of the Holy Spirit was upon Christ in a mighty way to minister to the needs of mankind:

"God ANOINTED Jesus of Nazareth with the Holy Spirit and with Power: Who went about doing good, and HEALING ALL that were oppressed of the Devil; for GOD WAS WITH HIM" (Acts 10:38).

The miracles that Christ performed and the power of His preaching came as a result of the ANOINTING. He ministered not as the *Son of God,* but as a *man* full of the Holy Spirit. If Christ had healed the lame, opened blinded eyes, and cleansed the leper as the *Son of God*, He would not have needed to be anointed! Who is able to anoint God?

The wonderful truth conveyed by the Ministry of Jesus Christ is that we can have the same power and anointing that He possessed, through the Baptism with the Holy Spirit. God gave the Spirit unto Christ *without measure* (Jn. 3:34), and Believers are promised this *same anointing,* with the accompanying signs and wonders, if they only will *believe* (Mk. 16:17-20; Jn. 7:37-39; 14:12-14; Acts 1:8; 2:4; etc.)

PURPOSE OF THIS DISPENSATION

The Purpose of God in the Dispensation of Grace was expressed by the words of Christ to Simon Peter:

"I say also unto you, That you are Peter, and upon this rock I WILL BUILD MY CHURCH; and the gates of Hell shall not prevail against it" (Mat. 16:18).

For this reason the Dispensation of Grace is often called the Church Age. The Christians in the Early Church understood the Plan of God for this Age, as it related to the Nation of Israel, for the Apostle James wrote:

"God at the first did visit the Gentiles, TO TAKE OUT OF THEM A PEOPLE FOR HIS NAME. And to this agree the words of the Prophets; as it is written, AFTER THIS (after the Church Age) *I WILL RETURN, AND WILL BUILD AGAIN THE TABERNACLE OF DAVID, WHICH IS FALLEN DOWN: AND I WILL BUILD AGAIN THE RUINS THEREOF, AND I WILL SET IT UP"* (Acts 15:14-16).

It is God's Plan during this Dispensation to *"call out"* (Greek, *ekklesia*) a people from all nations who have been Born-Again, Regenerated, Sanctified, Blood-washed, Blood-bought, identified with the Nature of Christ and the Plan of Redemption. The realization of this Divine program began with the earthly Ministry of Jesus Christ, for He announced the formation of the Church (Mat. 16:18). After the Church is completed and taken out of the world (Eph. 5:25-27; II Thess. 2:7), God once again will deal with Israel as a nation (Acts 15:16-17; Rom. 11:1-32).

CHURCH

As previously discussed, the New Testament Greek word for *"church"* is *ekklesia*, meaning *"an assembly of called-out ones."* This term is used to describe all of the Christians in a particular city (Acts 11:22; 13:1), a local congregation of Believers (I Cor. 14:19; Col. 4:15), and the entire Body of Christ on the Earth (Eph. 5:32).

Our English word *"church"* is derived from the Greek word *kyriakos*, which means, *"that which belongs to the Lord."* The Church is a company of people *"called out"* from the world, who have been Born-Again by the Spirit of God (Jn. 3:3-5) and who belong to the Lord Jesus Christ (Gal. 5:24).

BODY OF CHRIST

The Church is also called the Body of Christ (I Cor. 10:16; Eph. 4:12, etc.). Although Jesus left the Earth when He ascended into Heaven, He is still at work in the world through His Body, the Church. The Church is an *organism,* not a mere organization! The members of the Body and Christ relate to Christ as being His Body and members of His Flesh and Bones (Eph. 5:30). Christ is the Head of the Body in all things (Eph. 1:20-23; 5:23-27).

BRIDE OF CHRIST

What is the Bride of Christ?

The Bride of Christ is the Church, i.e., the *"Body of Christ."* The parable of the ten virgins portray the Bridegroom, Who is Christ, and the Bride, which is the Church (Mat. 25:1-13). John the Beloved wrote, *"He who has the Bride is the Bridegroom"* (Jn. 3:29). As is obvious here, Jesus is the Bridegroom and the Church, souls brought to Christ, constitute the *"Bride."* In Revelation, Chapter 21, the Scripture says, *"Come hither and I will show you the Bride, the Lamb's wife."* The Scripture then says, *"And he carried me away in the Spirit to a great and high mountain, and showed me that great city, the Holy Jerusalem, descending out of Heaven from God"* (Rev. 21:9-10).

The New Jerusalem will contain the Body of Christ, which is the Bride.

PURCHASE OF CHRIST

Jesus Christ purchased the Church with His Own Blood (Acts 20:28), and a person can become a part of the Church by having his sins washed away by the Blood of Christ (Rev. 1:5). The Atoning Work of Jesus Christ is a beautiful display of the Grace of God in this Dispensation! By the Sacrifice of Christ the penalty for sin was paid, and the Law was fulfilled. The demands of God for the Redemption of mankind were met at Calvary! All sinners now can be transformed by Faith in the Atonement, even as the thief who was crucified with Christ. To this one who said to Jesus, *"Lord, remember me when You come into Your Kingdom,"* Jesus replied:

"Verily I say unto you, Today shall you be with Me in Paradise" (Lk. 23:42-43).

This statement of Christ can be fully understood only by a discussion of the underworld of departed spirits.

UNDERWORLD OF DEPARTED SPIRITS

There are five separate places that comprise the underworld of departed spirits: (1) *tartaros,* (2) Paradise (Abraham's bosom), (3) Hell (Hades), (4) the bottomless pit (abyss), and (5) the Lake of Fire (gehenna).

TARTAROS

Tartaros, which is a Greek word translated *"Hell,"* is used only once in the New Testament, although references are made to this place in other Scriptures:

"God spared not the ANGELS WHO SINNED, but cast them down to HELL (tartaros)*, and delivered them into chains of darkness, to be reserved unto Judgment"* (II Pet. 2:4).

This prison of Hell is a special place of punishment for the fallen Angels that sinned:

"The SONS OF GOD (Angels) *saw the daughters of men that they were fair; and they took them wives of all which they chose"* (Gen. 6:2).

(For a complete discussion of this occurrence, study Chapter 6 of this Study Guide.) These wicked Angels in committing fornication with women were judged harshly by God:

"The Angels which kept not their first estate, but left their own habitation, He has reserved in EVERLASTING CHAINS UNDER DARKNESS unto the Judgment of the Great Day" (Jude, Vs. 6).

Tartaros is described as the deepest part of Hell. Jesus Christ descended into this place, and preached to the fallen Angels, after His Death on the Cross:

"Christ also has once suffered for sins. . . . also He went and PREACHED UNTO THE SPIRITS IN PRISON; Which sometime were disobedient, when once the longsuffering of God waited IN THE DAYS OF NOAH" (I Pet. 3:18-20).

Therefore, it is revealed that *tartaros* is a prison for the bound fallen angels (I Pet. 3:19), located under the Earth (II Pet. 2:4), a place of bondage for fallen Angels until their judgment (Jude, Vs. 6), a place visited by Christ when He descended into Hell (Ps. 16:10; I Pet. 3:19), a place of darkness (II Pet. 2:4; Jude, Vs. 6), a place of eternal fire (Jude, Vs. 7), and a place of vengeance (Jude, Vs. 7).

PARADISE (ABRAHAM'S BOSOM)

Paradise is described vividly in Luke 16:19-31, and also is called *"Abraham's bosom."* It was a place of comfort and bliss, located near

Hell, but was separated by a *"great gulf"* (Lk. 16:26). The wicked who were tormented in Hell could see those being comforted in Paradise (Lk. 16:23-25).

Before Calvary, Paradise was the abode of the Old Testament Saints after their death. All of the Righteous went into this prison and were held captive by the Devil (Heb. 2:14-15; Eph. 4:7-11). The Devil had the power of death and Hell before Christ conquered him (Col. 2:14-15; Rev. 1:18). After His Death on the Cross, Christ also descended into Paradise and released the Righteous souls held captive by Satan and took them to Heaven when He ascended on High:

"Wherefore he said, WHEN HE ASCENDED UP ON HIGH, HE LED CAPTIVITY CAPTIVE, and gave Gifts unto men. (Now that He ascended, what is it but that HE ALSO DESCENDED FIRST INTO THE LOWER PARTS OF THE EARTH? He Who descended is the same also Who ascended up far above all Heavens, that he might fill all things)" (Eph. 4:8-10).

This explains the reason why Jesus told the thief on the cross, *"Today shall you be with Me in Paradise"* (Lk. 23:43). It was into this place that the forgiven thief and Christ went the day they died. Paradise was located in the lower parts of the Earth (Eph. 4:9), next to Hell (Lk. 16:26). Christ was victorious over Satan, death, Hell, and the grave during His Crucifixion and during the three days He was in *tartaros* and Paradise. He now holds the keys to Hell and death:

"I AM HE WHO LIVES, AND WAS DEAD; AND, BEHOLD, I AM ALIVE FOR EVERMORE, AMEN; AND HAVE THE KEYS OF HELL AND OF DEATH" (Rev. 1:18).

Since the Work of Christ on Calvary, Christians now go immediately to Heaven when they die:

"We are confident, I say, and willing rather to be ABSENT FROM THE BODY, AND TO BE PRESENT WITH THE LORD" (II Cor. 5:8).

"I am in a strait betwixt two, having a desire to DEPART, AND TO BE WITH CHRIST; which is far better" (Phil. 1:23).

Since Christ led all of the Righteous souls out of Paradise into Heaven, it may be that Paradise continues, although empty, as a constant reminder to those in Hell of the Salvation and peace they forfeited by rejecting Christ (Lk. 16:23-31). It may also be that Hell spilled over into that area and *"enlarged herself"* (Isa. 5:14) ready to receive the millions of lost souls.

HELL (HADES)

Hell, or Hades, is the place of torment where all of the wicked spirits of men go at the moment of death. It will continue as the abode of all of the wicked from every Dispensation, until the end of the Millennium (Lk. 16:23-31). After the Millennium, the wicked will be resurrected from this place, to receive their immortal body and to be judged before the Great White Throne (Rev. 20:11-13; Jn. 5:29). After their Judgment the wicked will be cast into the Lake of Fire (Rev. 20:15).

BOTTOMLESS PIT (ABYSS)

The bottomless pit, or the abyss, is reserved for Satan, where he will be bound and cast during the Millennium (Rev. 20:1-3). No human ever will go to this place, for it is the abode of certain demons (Lk. 8:31) and fallen Angels (Rev. 9:1-3; 20:1-3). When Christ cast out the demons from the man of Gadara (Lk. 8:26-36), the demons begged Jesus not to cast them in the *"deep"* (Lk. 8:31), which is translated from the Greek *abussos* or *"bottomless pit"*. The bottomless pit is described as a horrible place:

"He opened the BOTTOMLESS PIT; and there arose a smoke out of the PIT, as the smoke of a great furnace; and the sun and the air were darkened by reason of the smoke of the PIT" (Rev. 9:2).

LAKE OF FIRE (GEHENNA)

The Lake of Fire, or gehenna, is the *eternal* Hell and final abode of every demon, fallen Angel, and man who ever has rebelled against God. The Lake of Fire was *"prepared for the Devil and his Angels"* (Mat. 25:41). The Beast and the False Prophet will be the first ones cast into this place prior to the Millennium (Rev. 20:10-15). The Lake of Fire is referred to as *"the second death"* (Rev. 20:14) and will be a place of everlasting:
1. FIRE (Mat. 5:22; Mk. 9:43);
2. THIRST (Lk. 16:24);
3. CONSCIOUSNESS (Lk. 16:24);
4. PAIN (Rev. 20:10);
5. DARKNESS (Mat. 22:13);
6. SORROWS AND WEEPING (Mat. 23:13);
7. MEMORY (Lk. 16:25); and,
8. HOPELESSNESS (Lk. 16:27-31).

The Scriptures teach that there will be varying degrees of punishment for the wicked, even as there will be varying degrees of rewards for the Righteous (Mat. 11:22; 12:38-42). Jesus Christ said that the Pharisees who devoured widows' houses and lived a hypocritical life would receive a *"greater damnation"* (Mk. 12:40).

"That servant, which knew his Lord's will, and prepared not himself, neither did according to His will, SHALL BE BEATEN WITH MANY

STRIPES. But he who knew not, and did commit things worthy of stripes, SHALL BE BEATEN WITH FEW STRIPES" (Lk. 12:47-48).

BLESSINGS OF THIS DISPENSATION

The test for mankind during the Dispensation of Grace is to have Faith in the Atoning Work of Christ and to believe His Promises! Obedience to *"the Law of Christ"* (Gal. 6:2; James 1:25; 2:8-12) through *"the Grace of God"* (Titus 2:11) is expected of every Believer.

SALVATION

The Blessings of God bestowed upon mankind during the Dispensation of Grace are too numerous to mention. However, we shall name a few.

Salvation is, of all the Blessings of God, the most wonderful! To be Born-Again is to become a New Creature in Christ and a Child of God.

The *New Birth* is the result of Repentance and Justification and Regeneration.

Repentance is both a condition and an act, for it is the state of being in Godly sorrow for sins committed and the act of turning from and forsaking those sins (II Cor. 7:10).

Justification is both a state and an act, for not only does God declare the Believer not guilty, but He views the Believer as though he never had committed a sin (Rom. 5:1-2; I Cor. 6:11)!

Regeneration is the communication of Divine life to the soul, and the impartation of a new nature, thus producing a New Creation in Christ (Jn. 3:5; II Pet. 1:4; I Jn. 5:11-13).

Sanctification is the separation of the Believer from that which is unholy, and the dedication of the Believer to the Service of the Lord (I Thess. 5:22-23; Rom. 12:1-2).

ONCE SAVED, ALWAYS SAVED?

The question often is asked, *"Is it possible for a Christian to backslide and lose his Salvation?"* Because the *"once saved, always saved"* doctrine of *unconditional* eternal security is so prevalent in the Church today, a person should know for certain what the Bible has to say on this important subject.

In Scripture, Salvation actually appears in three tenses — past, present, and future. We *were saved* from the guilt and penalty of sin (II Tim. 1:9; Titus 3:5) when we first believed. We *are being saved* from the power and dominion of sin (Rom. 6:14; 8:24; I Cor. 1:18) as we daily walk with God.

Ultimately we *shall be saved* from the penalty, power, and consequences of sin (Rom. 5:9-10; I Pet. 1:5). The Apostle Paul had the entire *process* of Salvation in view when he wrote:

"NOW is our Salvation nearer than WHEN WE (FIRST) BE-LIEVED" (Rom. 13:11).

We are not able to save ourselves by our own good works, as is so clearly taught in the Scriptures. Salvation is purely the *Grace* of God (Eph. 2:8-9). However, the Bible also declares that the evidence of a True Salvation experience is a life of *"Righteousness and True Holiness"* (Rom. 6:19-22; II Cor. 7:1; Eph. 4:24; I Thess. 3:13; 4:7). A life of Holiness is entirely possible by the power of the indwelling Christ (Rom. 8:15-16), for we become partakers of *His* Holiness (Heb. 12:10).

The Word of God solemnly warns that those persons who presume upon the Grace of God in continued sin and unrighteousness will forfeit their security in Christ:

"Make straight paths for your feet, lest that which is lame BE TURNED OUT OF THE WAY; but let it rather be healed. Follow peace with all men, AND HOLINESS, WITHOUT WHICH NO MAN SHALL SEE THE LORD: Looking diligently LEST ANY MAN FAIL OF THE GRACE OF GOD" (Heb. 12:13-15).

It should be noted that a Christian who backslides does so by willfully rejecting the Grace of God, *"that is able to keep (him) from falling"* (Gal. 5:4; I Pet. 1:5; Jude 24). This is the result of continued sin and rebellion, and the refusal to go before Jesus Christ, our *"Advocate with the Father"* to Repent of his sin and gain forgiveness (I Jn. 1:9; 2:1-2).

Therefore, it is stated explicitly in Scripture that it is possible for a Christian to *". . . receive the Word with joy; and these have no root, which FOR A WHILE believe, and IN TIME OF TEMPTATION FALL AWAY"* (Lk. 8:13).

The Apostle Paul recognized the necessity of reckoning daily the Grace of God in his own life, for he wrote:

"I keep under my body, and BRING IT INTO SUBJECTION: lest that by ANY MEANS, when I have preached to others, I MYSELF SHOULD BE A CASTAWAY" (I Cor. 9:27).

The writer of Hebrews warned his hearers:

"Therefore we ought to give the more earnest heed to the things which we have heard, lest any time WE SHOULD LET THEM SLIP . . . HOW SHALL WE ESCAPE, IF WE NEGLECT SO GREAT SALVA-TION?" (Heb. 2:1-3).

The Apostle James explained how to restore a Believer who has fallen into sin, and why the process of restoration is so important:

BRETHREN, if any of YOU do err from the Truth, and one

CONVERT him; Let him know, that he which converteth the sinner from the error of his way SHALL SAVE A SOUL FROM DEATH, AND SHALL HIDE A MULTITUDE OF SINS" (James 5:19-20).

The Apostle Peter gave the admonition that a Believer can be secure in Christ and never fall:

"Beside this, giving all diligence, add to your Faith Virtue; and to Virtue knowledge; And to knowledge temperance; and to temperance patience; and to patience godliness; And to godliness brotherly kindness; And to brotherly kindness charity. FOR IF THESE THINGS BE IN YOU AND ABOUND, THEY MAKE YOU THAT YOU SHALL NEITHER BE BARREN NOR UNFRUITFUL IN THE KNOWLEDGE OF OUR LORD JESUS CHRIST. But he who LACKS these things IS BLIND, and cannot see afar off, and HAS FORGOTTEN THAT HE WAS PURGED FROM HIS OLD SINS. Wherefore the rather, brethren, give diligence TO MAKE YOUR CALLING AND ELECTION SURE: FOR IF YOU DO THESE THINGS, YOU SHALL NEVER FALL: For so an entrance shall be Ministered unto you abundantly into the Everlasting Kingdom of our Lord and Saviour Jesus Christ" (II Pet. 1:5-11).

The eternal security of the Believer depends on a living relationship with Jesus Christ (Jn. 15:1-5). When a Believer chooses no longer to abide in Christ, he is cast away (Jn. 15:6; I Cor. 9:27). A person maintains his free moral agency both *before* and *after* his conversion experience. If he *makes the choice* to go back into a life of sin, he does so to the neglect of his soul's Salvation (Heb. 2:3), for the Bible makes it clear that it is possible for a man to have his name BLOTTED OUT of the Lamb's Book of Life (Ex. 32:33; Rev. 3:5; 22:19).

It is not the will of God that any of His sheep be lost, for Jesus promised that those sheep who *hear His Voice* and *follow Him* will be given *". . . Eternal Life; and they shall never perish, neither shall any man pluck them out of My Hand. My Father, which gave them to Me, is greater than all; and no man is able to pluck them out of my Father's Hand"* (Jn. 10:27-29).

However, when a Believer ceases to *follow Christ* and *hearken unto His Voice,* he cannot claim this wonderful promise. The Apostle Peter made it clear that a person is *"saved"* only as he *continues* to walk with God:

"For if AFTER they have ESCAPED the pollutions of the world THROUGH THE KNOWLEDGE OF THE LORD AND SAVIOUR JESUS CHRIST, THEY ARE AGAIN ENTANGLED THEREIN, AND OVERCOME, THE LATTER END IS WORSE WITH THEM THAN THE BEGINNING. For it had been BETTER FOR THEM NOT TO HAVE KNOWN THE WAY OF RIGHTEOUSNESS, THAN, AFTER THEY

*HAVE KNOWN IT, TO TURN FROM THE HOLY COMMANDMENT
DELIVERED UNTO THEM. But it is happened unto them according
to the true Proverb, The dog is turned to his own vomit again; and the
sow that was washed to her wallowing in the mire"* (II Pet. 2:20-22).

Therefore, the Bible teaches against the belief that it is impossible
for a person who once is Saved to be lost. But a person who is living in
right relationship with the Lord Jesus Christ should have no fear of losing
his Salvation.

*"This is the record, that God has given to us Eternal LIFE, and
this life is IN HIS SON"* (I Jn. 5:11).

BAPTISM WITH THE HOLY SPIRIT

The Baptism with the Holy Spirit is *"the Promise of the Father"* to
every Believer in the Dispensation of Grace (Acts 1:4; 2:38-39). There are
many different names for this glorious experience. It is called being *"filled
with the Holy Spirit"* (Acts 2:4), the *"Gift of the Holy Spirit"* (Acts
2:38), being *"Baptized with the Holy Spirit"* (Acts 1:5), and *"the Promise of the Father"* (Acts 1:4). The Baptism with the Holy Spirit is an
experience subsequent to the New Birth (Jn. 14:17; Acts 19:2).

PURPOSE OF THE BAPTISM WITH THE HOLY SPIRIT

The Purpose of the Baptism with the Holy Spirit is *primarily* to bestow, upon every Believer in this Dispensation, the power to fulfill the Great
Commission of the Lord Jesus Christ:

*"You shall receive POWER, after that the Holy Spirit is come upon
you: and you shall be WITNESSES unto Me both in Jerusalem, and in
all Judaea, and in Samaria, and UNTO THE UTTERMOST PART OF
THE EARTH"* (Acts 1:8).

Jesus made it clear to the Disciples that it was imperative that they
be Baptized with the Holy Spirit before going out to evangelize the
world (Lk. 24:49; Jn. 14:12-17; 16:7-15). The Baptism with the Holy
Spirit also brings the *full* enduement of the Spirit *without measure* (Jn.
7:37-39; 14:17).

While it is true that Old Testament Saints experienced various *"fill-
ings"* and *"Anointings"* of the Holy Spirit (I Sam. 16:13; II Chron. 15:1;
Lk. 1:41, 67), no person experienced the same Anointing of the Spirit that
was upon Jesus Christ during His earthly Ministry (Lk. 4:18; Jn. 3:34) until
after the Day of Pentecost (Acts 2:1-4).

Although every Believer receives the Holy Spirit at conversion (Rom.
8:14-16; I Cor. 12:3; Jn. 6:44), he does not receive the *fullness* of the

Spirit until he is Baptized *with the Holy Spirit* (Jn. 7: 37-39; Acts 1:5).

There are three Baptisms available to the New Testament Christian:

The *first Baptism* takes place when the Spirit of God baptizes a Believer into the Body of Christ (I Cor. 12:13). This occurs at the moment of the New Birth (Jn. 3:3-5).

The *second Baptism* available to the Believer is water baptism, when the minister immerses him in water as a symbol of his Baptism into the Body of Christ (Mat. 28:19; Acts 2:38).

The *third Baptism* available to the Believer comes when Jesus Christ Baptizes him into the Holy Spirit (Lk. 3:14; Acts 1:5; 2:4).

Baptism into Christ is essential to *Salvation* (Gal. 3:27). Baptism in water is essential to *obedience* (Mat. 3:25-26; I Pet. 3:21). Baptism with the Holy Spirit is essential to *receiving power to do the Works of Christ* (Lk. 24:49; Jn. 14:12-17).

BENEFITS OF THE BAPTISM WITH THE HOLY SPIRIT

Other benefits of being Baptized with the Holy Spirit include the following:

1. THE SPIRIT HELPING OUR INFIRMITIES AND WEAKNESSES (Rom. 8:26);

2. AN INTENSIFIED PRAYER LIFE (Rom. 8:26; Jude, Vs. 20);

3. THE ABILITY TO DO THE GREATER WORKS OF CHRIST (Jn. 14:12);

4. A GREATER REVELATION OF CHRIST AND HIS WORD (Jn. 14:26; 16:13-14);

5. AN INCREASE IN THE LEVEL OF FAITH IN A BELIEVER'S LIFE (Jude, Vs. 20);

6. A REFRESHING AND REST FOR THE WEARY (Isa. 28:11-12);

7. PERSONAL EDIFICATION (I Cor. 14:4);

8. A GATEWAY TO ALL OF THE GIFTS OF THE SPIRIT (I Cor. 12:7-11);

9. POWER TO RESIST THE DEVIL AND TEMPTATION (Gal. 5:16; James 4:7); and,

10. A MORE ACTIVE LOVE FOR CHRIST, FOR HIS WORD, AND FOR THE LOST (Acts 4:24-37; 5:29; I Cor. 14:1).

CONDITIONS TO RECEIVING THE BAPTISM WITH THE HOLY SPIRIT

Conditions for being Baptized with the Holy Spirit are *Salvation*

(Jn. 14:17; Acts 19:2), *Faith* (Gal. 3:14), *asking God* (Lk. 11:13), and *receiving* (Acts 8:17; 10:47). God has promised in His Word that those who *"hunger and thirst after Righteousness . . . SHALL BE FILLED"* (Mat. 5:6).

EVIDENCE OF THE BAPTISM WITH THE HOLY SPIRIT

Evidence that a person had been filled with the Holy Spirit in Old Testament times was primarily that of *Prophecy* (Num. 11:25; I Sam. 10:10; Lk. 1:41-44, 67). However, the Prophet Isaiah, hundreds of years before Pentecost, foretold that God, in this Dispensation, would give a new evidence that a person had received the fullness of the Spirit:

"Whom shall he teach knowledge? and whom shall he make to understand doctrine?. . . FOR WITH STAMMERING LIPS AND ANOTHER TONGUE WILL HE SPEAK TO THIS PEOPLE. To whom He said, This is the rest wherewith you may cause the weary to rest; and this is the refreshing: yet they would not hear" (Isa. 28:9-12).

When the 120 Believers were Baptized with the Holy Spirit on the Day of Pentecost, this Prophecy was fulfilled:

"They were ALL filled with the Holy Spirit, and began TO SPEAK WITH OTHER TONGUES, as the Spirit gave them utterance" (Acts 2:4).

Speaking with other tongues continued as the initial evidence of the Baptism with the Holy Spirit throughout the Book of Acts (Acts 2:4; 10:46; 11:15; 19:6). It continues today as the Bible evidence that a person *truly* has been filled with the Holy Spirit, for we are in the *same Dispensation* as the First-Century Church! *God has not changed His program*!

One of the most convincing proofs that speaking with other tongues is the initial, physical evidence of the Baptism with the Holy Spirit (besides Scripture) is that when a *deaf mute* is filled with the Spirit, he too speaks in other tongues as the Spirit gives him the supernatural utterance!

PENTECOSTAL EVANGELISM

In these last days God has promised to pour out His Spirit upon *all flesh* (Acts 2:17), and this Prophecy is being fulfilled around the world! Pentecostals are the leading missionary force, taking the Gospel to every creature (Mk. 16:15). Jesus said:

"THIS GOSPEL (of Salvation, Holy Spirit Baptism, Divine healing, and the Second Coming of Christ) *of the Kingdom shall be preached in all the world for a witness unto ALL NATIONS; and then shall the end come"* (Mat. 24:14).

The *known* world has been evangelized only once, and that in the days of the Apostles (Mk. 16:17-20; Acts 17:6; Rom. 1:8). The world was evangelized the first and only time by *Pentecostals*, and it will be evangelized the *second* time by *Pentecostals*! The fulfillment of the Great Commission is possible only when Believers are *"endued with Power from on High"* (Lk. 24:49) to complete this awesome responsibility!

SELF-HELP
STUDY NOTES

DIVINE HEALING

Another great Blessing God has bestowed during the Dispensation of Grace is *Divine healing*. God manifested His Healing Power under the Old Covenant (Ex. 15:26; Num. 12:13-15; Ps. 105:37), and because we are living under a *"BETTER Covenant . . . established upon BETTER promises"* (Heb. 8:6), we can rejoice that God still heals the sick *today*!

Sickness and death came upon the human race because of sin (Rom. 5:12) and is actually a curse upon fallen mankind (Ex. 15:26; Deut. 28:15-68). Satan is the author of disease and death, and Christ came to Earth to *"destroy the works of the Devil"* (Acts 10:38, I Jn. 3:8).

When Jesus died on the Cross, the Atonement made full provision for our physical healing, as well as our deliverance from the guilt, penalty, and power of sin (Isa. 53:4-5; Mat. 8:17; I Pet. 2:24). The benefits of the Atonement can be appropriated only by *Faith* — and in no other way.

When Jesus asked a person, *"Do YOU believe that I am able to do this?"* (Mat. 9:28) or *"What will YOU that I should do unto you?"* (Mk. 10:51), He responded to their answer, *"According to YOUR FAITH be it unto you"* (Mat. 9:29) or *"Go your way; YOUR FAITH has made you whole"* (Mk. 10:52).

It is always God's Will to heal, for it was not His Will that sin, sickness, and disease ever should have come into the world! Jesus Christ healed everyone who came to Him seeking healing (Mat. 8:16; 12:15; Lk. 4:40; 6:19; Acts 10:38). And the Bible clearly teaches that:

"Jesus Christ (is) *the SAME yesterday, and today, and forever"* (Heb. 13:8).

Jesus committed the healing ministry first of all to the Twelve (Mat. 10:1), to the Seventy (Lk. 10:8-9), and finally to every Believer:

"These signs shall follow them who BELIEVE . . . THEY SHALL LAY HANDS ON THE SICK, AND THEY SHALL RECOVER" (Mk. 16:17-18).

"Is any sick among you? let him call for the Elders of the Church; and let them pray over him, anointing him with oil in the Name of the Lord: AND THE PRAYER OF FAITH SHALL SAVE THE SICK, AND THE LORD SHALL RAISE HIM UP" (James 5:14-15).

Even as Moses lifted up the serpent in the wilderness, bringing healing to the children of Israel (Num. 21:8-9), so Christ was lifted up on the Cross (Jn. 3:14) bringing healing to every Believer! The children of Israel were required only to *look* at the serpent to be healed, and we receive healing in the same manner today by *". . . LOOKING UNTO JESUS the Author and Finisher of our FAITH"* (Heb. 1:2).

It is certain that we do not understand everything there is to know about Divine Healing, *"for now we see through a glass, darkly"* (I Cor. 13:12). Why some people are healed, while others are not . . . why one who possesses little or no obvious faith is delivered, while a faithful saint of God dies . . . are questions for which we have no complete answers.

"The secret things belong unto the LORD our God: but those things which are revealed belong to us" (Deut. 29:29).

One thing IS for certain. God has *commanded* us *to pray* for the sick, in *faith believing*, and to leave the *results* in His Hands (Mk. 16:17-18; James 5:14-15).

OTHER BENEFITS

The other benefits God has given to Believers in the Dispensation of Grace includes answers to prayer (Mat. 6:4-6; Mk. 11:22-24; Jn. 14:12-15), physical and spiritual prosperity (Mat. 6:25-33; Phil. 4:19; III Jn., Vs. 2), the unlimited Power of God (Mat. 17:19-21; Mk. 9:23), and the hope of Eternal Life (Jn. 14:1-3, Titus 1:2; 3:7).

HISTORY OF THE EARLY CHURCH

While the history of the Early Church reveals the continuation of the Blessings of God throughout the Apostolic Age, there began to be failure and apostasy (Acts 5:1-11; Gal. 5:5-9; I Tim. 1:19-20; II Tim. 4:10). The apostasy that began in the Apostolic Age continued to increase through the Centuries until the Power of God in the Church was almost a thing of the past. The Church entered the Dark Ages and corruption increased. The bishops of the Church began to rule through Civil Government and murdered millions of people because they would not conform to the Roman Catholic religion. With the exception of a few isolated spiritual awakenings, the power of Pentecost had been almost totally extinguished.

PROTESTANT REFORMATION

Then Martin Luther began the Protestant Reformation by declaring that *"the just shall live by his faith"* (Hab. 2:4). Once the Bible Doctrine of Salvation by Grace had been restored, the Spirit of God began flaming the fires of revival! The Bible once again was read by the common man. The Anabaptists began teaching water baptism by immersion. John Wesley began preaching Sanctification and a life of Holiness. A fervent expectancy for the soon return of the Lord swept the heart and life of Believers.

PENTECOSTAL REVIVAL

Then at the turn of the Twentieth Century, a group of Bible college students in Topeka, Kansas, began seeking the reality of the Baptism with the Holy Spirit. On New Year's Day, 1901, God poured out His Spirit upon these searching hearts, and they began to speak with other tongues! The Pentecostal revival spread quickly across the nation and around the world. The full restoration of the New Testament Church had become a reality!

FUTURE OF THIS DISPENSATION

The Dispensation of Grace, which began with the Life and Ministry of Jesus Christ, continues today! The future events of this Dispensation are revealed clearly in the Word of God. God promised that Israel would be restored as a nation in the land of Palestine (Jer. 31:35-36; Ezek. 37:21). The formation of the new state of Israel on May 14, 1948, was a giant step toward the fulfillment of this Prophecy!

RAPTURE OF THE CHURCH

The next event scheduled to occur during this Dispensation, according to Bible Prophecy, is the Rapture of the Church (Lk. 21:34-36; Jn. 14:1-3; I Cor. 15:23, 51-58; Phil. 3:20-21; Col. 3:4; I Thess. 4:13-17). While the word *"rapture"* is not found in the Bible, it certainly conveys the truth of this glorious event. Paul referred to the Rapture as the *"blessed hope"* of the Church:

"Looking for that Blessed Hope, and the glorious appearing of the Great God and our Saviour Jesus Christ" (Titus 2:13).

This Scripture and others reveal that the New Testament Saints were looking for this event to occur in their day, providing that the Rapture could occur at any moment. The most vivid description of the Rapture of the Church is given in Paul's First Epistle to the Thessalonians:

"For the Lord Himself shall descend from Heaven with a shout, with the voice of the Archangel, and with the Trump of God: and the dead in Christ shall rise first: Then we which are alive and remain shall be caught up together with them in the clouds, to meet the Lord

in the air: and so shall we ever be with the Lord" (I Thess. 4:16-17).

PURPOSE OF THE RAPTURE

The Purpose of the Rapture will be to resurrect all of the righteous dead, from each Dispensation, reuniting the soul and spirit with a glorified body (I Cor. 15:35-55). They then will be caught up, along with all of the Saints still living on the Earth, to meet the Lord in the air and return with Him to Heaven (Jn. 14:1-3).

PRE-TRIBULATION

The Rapture will occur *before* the Great Tribulation as taught by several Scriptures:

"Watch ye therefore, and pray always, that you may be accounted worthy TO ESCAPE ALL THESE THINGS (the Tribulation) that shall come to pass, and to stand before the Son of man" (Lk. 21:36).

"For God has not appointed us to WRATH (the Tribulation), but to obtain SALVATION by our Lord Jesus Christ" (I Thess. 5:9).

"The mystery of iniquity does already work: only he (the Church) who now lets will let, until he be TAKEN OUT OF THE WAY. AND THEN shall that Wicked be revealed" (II Thess. 2:7-8).

"After this I looked, and, behold, A DOOR WAS OPENED IN HEAVEN: and the first voice which I heard was as it were of a trumpet talking with me; which said, COME UP HITHER, AND I WILL SHOW YOU THINGS WHICH MUST BE HEREAFTER (after the Rapture of the Church)" (Rev. 4:1).

While the Church is mentioned 17 times in the first three Chapters of the Book of Revelation, it is NEVER MENTIONED AGAIN as being on the Earth, but is immediately pictured as being in Heaven (Rev. 4:1-11). The inhabitants of the Earth then will experience the most horrible time in history (Mat. 24:21), followed by the Second Coming of Christ WITH the Saints (Mat. 24:29-30; Jude, Vs. 14; Rev. 19:11-21).

CONTRAST BETWEEN RAPTURE AND SECOND COMING

While the Earth is going through the Great Tribulation, the Saints of God will be in Heaven, to stand before the Judgment Seat of Christ (Rom. 14:10; II Cor. 5:10) and to attend the Marriage Supper of the Lamb (Mat. 26:29; Rev. 19:7-9).

Many people do not distinguish between the Rapture of the Church and the Second Coming of Christ. The chart below gives a brief contrast:

RAPTURE OF THE CHURCH	SECOND COMING OF CHRIST
1. It occurs *before* the Tribulation (Lk. 21:36).	1. It occurs *after* the Tribulation (Mat. 24:29-30).
2. Christ comes *for* the Saints (I Thess. 4:13-17).	2. Christ comes *with* the Saints (Jude, Vs. 14; Rev. 19:11-21).
3. Christ takes the Saints to *Heaven* (Jn. 14:3).	3. Christ brings the Saints back to Earth (Zech. 14:4-5; Rev. 19:14).
4. Christ returns to the *clouds* (I Thess. 4:17).	4. Christ returns to the *Earth* (Zech. 14:4-5).
5. Christ is not seen (I Cor. 15:52).	5. Every eye shall see Christ (Rev. 1:7).
6. It is the *"blessed hope"* of the Church (Titus 2:13).	6. It is the great day of His *"wrath"* (Rev. 19:15).

JUDGMENT SEAT OF CHRIST

The purpose of the Judgment Seat of Christ will be to judge the *works* of every Believer from each Dispensation:

"Now if any man build upon this foundation gold, silver, precious stones, wood, hay, stubble; EVERY MAN'S WORK SHALL BE MADE MANIFEST: for the day shall declare it, because IT SHALL BE RE-VEALED BY FIRE; AND THE FIRE SHALL TRY EVERY MAN'S WORK OF WHAT SORT IT IS. If any man's work ABIDE which he has built thereupon, HE SHALL RECEIVE A REWARD. If any man's work shall BE BURNED, HE SHALL SUFFER LOSS: but he himself shall be SAVED; yet so as by fire" (I Cor. 3:12-15).

The judgment of the Believer's *sins* is already past, for Jesus bore our sins in His Body on the Cross at Calvary. Our sins *never* will be brought to our account again, for they have been *forgiven* and *forgotten* (Isa. 43:25; I Pet. 2:24). However, a careful ledger has been kept of *every* work the Believer has performed since he has become a Christian (Mat. 12:36; Rom. 14:12; II Cor. 5:10). Believers will be judged on the basis of their . . .

1. DOCTRINAL BELIEFS — true or false (Rom. 2:14-16; 14:1-10),

2. CONDUCT TOWARD OTHERS — kind or unkind (Mat. 18:10; Mk. 9:41; II Tim. 4:14),

3. STEWARDSHIP — faithful or unfaithful (Mat. 25:14-29; Lk. 12:42-44; I Cor. 4:1-5),

4. WORDS — good or bad (Mat. 12:36-37; Eph. 4:19),

5. TALENTS — used or wasted (Mat. 5:15-16; Mk. 4:25),

6. ATTITUDES — Christlike or selfish (Mat. 6:1-7; Eph. 4:30-32),

7. MOTIVES — right or wrong (Mat. 6:16-18; Lk. 14:12-14),

8. TRAITS — spiritual or carnal (Rom. 2:1-6; Col. 3:8-16),

9. EVERY DEED — worthy or worthless (Mk. 9:41; Col. 3:23-25).

The deeds performed in a worthy manner will be rewarded, but those deeds Christ judges unworthy will be burned and will cause the Believer lost rewards (I Cor. 3:12-15).

The following rewards have been promised for faithful service to the Lord:

1. VICTOR'S CROWN (I Cor. 9:25);

2. CROWN OF RIGHTEOUSNESS (II Tim. 4:8);

3. CROWN OF REJOICING (I Thess. 2:19);

4. CROWN OF LIFE (James 1:12);

5. CROWN OF GLORY (I Pet. 5:4);

6. MARTYR'S CROWN (Rev. 2:10); and,

7. CROWN OF GOLD (Rev. 4:4).

Saints will be given a mansion in which to live eternally (Jn. 14:2), and Christ also will determine the amount of earthly rulership given to each Saint on the basis of his faithfulness to God in this present life (Lk. 19:12-26); for we shall reign as kings and priests with Christ forever (Rev. 1:6; 5:10). Because the Scriptures clearly indicate that it is possible for someone else to take our crown (Rev. 3:11), it behooves every Christian to be diligent in his service to the King of kings!

MARRIAGE SUPPER
OF THE LAMB

Following the Judgment Seat of Christ will be the Marriage Supper of the Lamb and all the redeemed from every Dispensation who will live in the New Jerusalem, which is the Bride of Christ (Rev. 19:7-9; 21:9-10). John the Revelator wrote:

"Let us be glad and rejoice, and give honour to Him: for the MARRIAGE OF THE LAMB IS COME, and his wife has made herself ready. And to her was granted that she should be arrayed in fine linen, clean and white: for the fine linen is the Righteousness of Saints. And he said unto me, Write, BLESSED ARE THEY WHICH ARE CALLED

UNTO THE MARRIAGE SUPPER OF THE LAMB" (Rev. 19:7-9).

This is the only reference in the entire Bible to this glorious event, which will occur toward the end of the Great Tribulation when God will resurrect the Saints who have been martyred (Rev. 7:9-17) during this time. They will join with us as we sit down together at the Master's table! This will be a literal banquet, for it is revealed that we shall eat food, in our glorified body, even as we do now (Lk. 24:36-43; Rev. 2:7, 17; 22:1-2).

TRIBULATION ON EARTH

While the Saints of God are enjoying the splendor of Heaven, for seven years, the condition of the Earth will be yet another story! After the Rapture of the Church from this Planet the Antichrist will be revealed (II Thess. 2:1-12).

FORMATION OF TEN KINGDOMS AND REVELATION OF ANTICHRIST

Just prior to the Antichrist's rise to power, the nations that presently exist inside the Old Roman Empire will be reduced to 10 separate kingdoms ruled by 10 separate kings (Dan. 7:7-8, 19, 25). The countries presently existing inside the Old Roman Empire include England, France, Belgium, Switzerland, Holland, Spain, Portugal, Italy, Austria, Hungary, Romania, Yugoslavia, Bulgaria, Albania, Greece, Turkey, Syria, Lebanon, Egypt, Iraq, Iran, Libya, Algeria, Tunisia, and Morocco. Through wars, treaties, and/or alliances these nations will become 10 separate kingdoms with 10 separate leaders.

After the 10 kingdoms have existed for a short time independent of the Antichrist (Dan. 7:7, 23-24; Rev. 12:12; 17:10), he then will arise from the Syrian division. In the first 3-1/2 years of the Tribulation he will conquer Greece, Turkey, and Egypt, thus reviving the Old Grecian Empire into one empire. By this time the other six kingdoms of the 10 will give him their power without any further war (Rev. 17:8-17).

ANTICHRIST'S COVENANT WITH ISRAEL

The Antichrist will make a seven-year Covenant with the nation of Israel, who will receive him as her *"messiah"* (Dan. 9:27; Jn. 5:43). The Jewish Temple will be rebuilt in Jerusalem, either before or shortly after this time, and the reinstitution of the animal sacrifice will occur (Dan. 9:27; Mat. 24:15; Rev. 11:1-2).

EXTENT OF ANTICHRIST'S KINGDOM

While the Antichrist is continuing his conquest, the countries north and east of the 10 kingdoms, including Russia and Germany, will plan an attack against his military strategy (Ezek., Chpts. 38-39; Dan. 11:44). In the middle of the Tribulation war will be declared by the countries north and east of his kingdom (Dan. 11:44). The Antichrist will conquer Russia and her allies and then will become the *"prince of Meshech and Tubal"* (Ezek., Chpts. 38-39).

This will be the fullest extent of the Antichrist's kingdom. He will *not* be a worldwide dictator, for even a few if the countries *bordering* on his kingdom will not succumb to his power:

"He shall enter also into the glorious land, and many countries shall be overthrown: BUT THESE SHALL ESCAPE OUT OF HIS HAND, EVEN EDOM, AND MOAB, AND THE CHIEF OF THE CHILDREN OF AMMON" (Dan. 11:41).

The Antichrist *will* rule over the entire world known to man during the days of the Old Roman Empire (Dan. 2:42-44; 7:24; Rev. 13:1-8), but this was an area limited to the nations listed above.

SEAL JUDGMENTS

The seven Seal Judgments mentioned in the Book of Revelation will occur toward the beginning of the Great Tribulation:

1. FIRST SEAL — rise of the Antichrist (Rev. 6:1-2);
2. SECOND SEAL — war (Rev. 6:3-4);
3. THIRD SEAL — famine (Rev. 6:5-6);
4. FOURTH SEAL — death and Hell (Rev. 6:7-8);
5. FIFTH SEAL — martyrdom of Saints (Rev. 6:9-11);
6. SIXTH SEAL — wrath of God (Rev. 6:12-17); and,
7. SEVENTH SEAL — silence in Heaven for one-half hour (Rev. 8:1).

TRUMPET JUDGMENTS

These are followed by the seven Trumpet Judgments:

1. FIRST TRUMPET — hail, fire, and blood (Rev. 8:7);
2. SECOND TRUMPET — one-third of the sea turned to blood (Rev. 8:8-9);
3. THIRD TRUMPET — drinking waters poisoned (Rev. 8:10-11);
4. FOURTH TRUMPET — one-third of the planets darkened (Rev. 8:12);

5. FIFTH TRUMPET — men tormented by demon locusts (Rev. 9:1-12);

6. SIXTH TRUMPET — one-third of men killed (Rev. 9:13-21); and,

7. SEVENTH TRUMPET — Satan cast out of Heaven (Rev. 11:15-19; 12:7-12).

PURPOSE OF THE TRIBULATION

Just prior to the Trumpet Judgments, God will seal 144,000 Jews, 12,000 from each of the 12 tribes of Israel, and will protect them from the Trumpet Judgments (Rev. 7:1-8; 9:4). The purpose of the Tribulation will be to purify Israel and bring them back to a place of Repentance where God can fulfill the Covenants He made with their fathers (Isa. 24:1-23; Ezek. 20:33-34; Rom. 11:25-29).

EVENTS OF THE MIDDLE OF THE TRIBULATION

In the middle of the seven years several events will take place. The Antichrist will break his Covenant with Israel, invade Jerusalem, defile the Temple, and set himself up to be worshipped (Dan. 9:27; Mat. 24:15; II Thess. 2:4). The Temple at Jerusalem will become the capital building for the Antichrist's kingdom during the last 3-1/2 years of the Tribulation. Also at this time the two witnesses, Enoch and Elijah, will appear on the Earth. They will protect Israel against her enemies, and will preach the Gospel, until they are killed, resurrected, and received back into Heaven (Zech. 4:11-14; Mal. 4:5; Heb. 9:27; Rev. 11:3-12). God also will translate the 144,000 Jews, known as the manchild, in the middle of the Tribulation at the conclusion of their mission (Rev. 7:1-8; 12:5; 14:1-5).

GREAT TRIBULATION

It is at this point that the second half of the Tribulation, referred to as the Great Tribulation, will begin. Israel will flee into the countries of Edom and Moab for the last 3-1/2 years of the Great Tribulation, where she will be protected from the Antichrist (Ezek. 20:33-39; Dan. 11:40-45; Mat. 24:15-21; Rev. 12:6, 13-17). When Israel flees, the armies of the Antichrist will attempt to retrieve her, but will be swallowed by the Earth (Rev. 12:13-16).

MARK OF THE BEAST

When the Antichrist defiles the Jewish Temple, setting up his image to be worshipped, another man, known as the False Prophet, will institute this new religious worship (Rev. 13:11-18; 16:13-14). The citizens of the kingdom of the Antichrist who refuse to worship the beast, and receive his mark, name, and/or the number of his name will be beheaded (Rev. 13:11-18; 14:9-11; 20:4). Those who do receive the mark, name, or number of the beast will be lost eternally (Rev. 14:9-11). We do not know what the mark or name of the beast will be, but the number will be 666 (Rev. 13:18), and it will not be given until the second half of the Great Tribulation.

SALVATION DURING THE TRIBULATION

That people will be Saved during the Tribulation is clear from several Scriptures (Rev. 7:9-17; 12:11; Zech. 12:10). The Apostle Peter, quoting from the Prophet Joel, stated:

"It shall come to pass IN THE LAST DAYS, SAITH GOD, I WILL POUR OUT OF MY SPIRIT UPON ALL FLESH . . . The sun shall be turned into darkness, and the moon into blood, before that great and notable Day of the Lord come: And it shall come to pass, that WHO-SOEVER SHALL CALL ON THE NAME OF THE LORD SHALL BE SAVED" (Acts 2:17-21).

Jesus promised that the Holy Spirit would *"abide"* on the Earth *"forever"* (Jn. 14:16) and would be poured out during these last days (Acts 2:17). The Holy Spirit will anoint the two witnesses (Rev. 11:3-11), and the Gospel shall be preached by them, the Tribulation Saints, and the Messenger Angel (Rev. 14:6-7). Everyone who believes the Gospel message will be Born-Again (Jn. 3:3-5), although it will cost many their life (Rev. 20:4). Although the Tribulation primarily will be a time of judgment, the Grace of God still will be manifested to His people, for this period will come at the close of the Dispensation of Grace.

VIAL JUDGMENTS

When the seven Vial Judgments are poured out, the Great Tribulation will be swiftly closing:

1.   FIRST VIAL — malignant sores upon those who take the mark of the beast (Rev. 16:2);

2.   SECOND VIAL — sea turned to blood (Rev. 16:3);

3.   THIRD VIAL — rivers turned to blood (Rev. 16:4-7);

4.   FOURTH VIAL — men scorched by sun (Rev. 16:8-9);

5.   FIFTH VIAL — Antichrist's kingdom covered by darkness (Rev. 16:10-11);

6.   SIXTH VIAL — Euphrates River dried up (Rev. 16:12); and,

7.   SEVENTH VIAL — great earthquake and 100-pound hailstones (Rev. 16:17-21).

Jesus Christ said that *"except those days should be shortened,"* no flesh would survive this horrible time (Mat. 24:22), but *"for the elect's sake* (Israel)*"* God will bring a halt to this persecution.

BATTLE OF ARMAGEDDON

In the final days of the Great Tribulation Israel will regain possession of Jerusalem, by the help of God and the two witnesses. The Antichrist then will return with the armies of his kingdom and the nations he has conquered, including Russia (Ezek., Chpts. 38-39; Dan. 11:44). He will regain Jerusalem and take half of the city captive (Zech. 14:1-9). Then Christ will appear suddenly from Heaven with all His raptured Saints and His Angels, and will defeat the Antichrist and all of his armies in one day of battle — the Battle of Armageddon (Ezek., Chpts. 38-39; Zech. 14:1-9; Rev. 19:11-21). This is the Second Coming of Christ (Mat. 24:29-31), when the Nation of Israel will be saved in a single day (Isa. 66:7-8; Zech. 12:10; Mat. 23:37-39; Rom. 11:25-29).

The Battle of Armageddon will be the worst conflict in the history of the world. The bloodshed will be so vast that the blood will flow to the horse's bridles (Rev. 14:20). The Antichrist and the False Prophet will be killed in this battle (II Thess. 2:8-9), then resurrected to be cast into the Lake of Fire (Dan. 7:11; Rev. 19:20) forever. Satan then will be bound and cast into the bottomless pit for 1,000 years (Rev. 20:1-3).

JUDGMENT OF THE NATIONS

Following this Christ will judge all of the Gentile nations on the basis of how they treated Christ's brethren — the Jews (Mat. 25:31-46). He will separate the sheep nations, which were kind to Israel, from the goat nations, which persecuted Israel. The goat nations will be sent to Hell (Mat. 25:41), while the sheep nations will be allowed to inhabit the Earth, in their natural body, throughout the Millennium (Mat. 25:34) and the Eternal Ages (Rev. 21:24), providing they do not rebel with Satan at the end of the Millennium (Rev. 20:3-9), when he is loosed for *"a little season."*

MILLENNIAL KINGDOM

After this Christ will set up His Millennial Kingdom on the Earth for

1,000 years of peace. This will come as a tranquil calm after a violent storm! What a glorious event it will be when Jesus comes back to Earth again!

> *"Oh! Our Lord is coming back to Earth again!*
> *"Yes, our Lord is coming back to Earth again!*
> *"Satan will be bound a thousand years,*
> *"We'll have no tempter then!*
> *"After Jesus shall come back to Earth again!"*

Chapter 11

The Dispensation Of Divine Government — The Millennium

CHAPTER ELEVEN

THE DISPENSATION OF DIVINE GOVERNMENT — THE MILLENNIUM

From the Binding of Satan to the Renovation of the Heavens and Earth (Rev. 20:1-15)

ISRAEL PROMISED A KINGDOM

Both the Abrahamic Covenant and the Davidic Covenant promised that Israel would have an everlasting earthly kingdom through which all of the families of the Earth would be blessed (Gen. 12:1-3; 13:14-17; 17:6-8; II Sam. 7:8-17; Ps. 89:3-4, 20-37).

That is the reason why the Jews were looking for a King as their Messiah, the Prince of *"the house of David."* They blindly overlooked the prophecies concerning His First Coming into the world as a suffering Savior, because there are so many more prophecies of His earthly Reign!

From Genesis to Malachi there is a note of praise, as lawgiver and historian, psalmist and prophet constantly refer to the Kingdom Age, when the Messiah shall Reign.

From Matthew to Revelation the hope continues as John the Baptist, Jesus Christ, and all of the Apostles preach the Gospel of the Kingdom. The Prophecy went forth in the Early Church how *". . . God at the first did visit the Gentiles, to take out of them a people for His Name* (the Church). *. . . After this* (the Dispensation of Grace) *I WILL RETURN, AND WILL BUILD AGAIN THE TABERNACLE OF DAVID, which is fallen down; and I WILL BUILD AGAIN THE RUINS THEREOF, AND I WILL SET IT UP: That the residue of men might seek after the Lord, and all the Gentiles, upon whom My Name is called, saith the Lord, Who does all these things"* (Acts 15:14-17).

This Golden Age, known as the Millennium, will surely come to pass, for *"all the Promises of God in Him are yes, and in Him Amen"* (II Cor. 1:20).

LENGTH OF THIS DISPENSATION

The Millennium will be the last Dispensation of mankind before the eternal perfect state. This era of human history is referred to as the

Dispensation of Divine Government because the eternal Triune God will set up an eternal kingdom over which He will rule the nations of the Earth forever.

The word *"millennium"* is derived from two Latin words, *mille* (*"thousand"*) and *annum* (*"year"*). Although *"millennium"* is not stated in Scripture, the phrase *"thousand years"* is mentioned six times in Revelation 20:1-15.

NAMES FOR THE MILLENNIUM

Scriptures also refer to the Millennium as follows:

1. THE DISPENSATION OF THE FULLNESS OF TIME (Eph. 1:10)
2. THE WORLD [GREEK *AION*, *"AGE"*] TO COME (Mat. 12:32; Mk. 10:30; Lk. 20:35; Eph. 1:21; 2:7)
3. THE KINGDOM OF GOD (Mk. 14:25; Lk. 10:11; 22:14-18)
4. THE KINGDOM OF OUR LORD AND OF HIS CHRIST (Rev. 11:15)
5. THE KINGDOM OF HEAVEN (Mat. 7:21; 8:11; 10:7)
6. THE KINGDOM OF THEIR FATHER (Mat. 13:43)
7. THE DAY OF THE LORD (Isa. 2:12; Zech. 14:1; II Pet. 3:10)
8. THAT DAY (Isa. 4:1-6; 26:1-3; Hos. 2:18; Joel 3:18; Zech. 12:8-9)
9. THE REGENERATION (Mat. 19:28)
10. THE TIMES OF REFRESHING (Acts 3:19)
11. THE TIMES OF RESTITUTION OF ALL THINGS (Acts 3:21)
12. THE CONSOLATION OF ISRAEL (Lk. 2:25)

PURPOSE OF THIS DISPENSATION

These designations also reveal the purpose of the Millennium, which will last from the binding of Satan to the renovation of the New Heavens and New Earth (II Pet. 3:10-13; Rev. 21:1):

"I saw an Angel come down from Heaven, having the key of the bottomless pit and a great chain in his hand. And he laid hold on the dragon, that old serpent, which is the Devil, and Satan, and BOUND HIM A THOUSAND YEARS, And cast him into the bottomless pit, and shut him up, and set a seal upon him, that he should deceive the nations no more, till the THOUSAND YEARS should be fulfilled: and after that he must be loosed a little season" (Rev. 20:1-3).

The entire program of God during this Dispensation will be to put down all rebellion in the Earth so that God may rule as He did before the Fall (I Cor. 15:24-28). He will do this by exalting the Saints to rule as kings and priests, according to the reward of their works (I Cor. 3:11-15; II Cor. 5:10; Rev. 1:5; 20:4-6).

By fulfilling His eternal Covenants made with Abraham, Isaac, Jacob, and David, God will restore Israel to the Promised Land, where she will be the head of the nations (Deut. 28:1-14; Ezek. 20:33-44; Chpts. 38-39; Acts 15:13-17). Christ will reign over the world in Righteousness, restoring the original Plan of God for mankind (Isa. 2:2-5; 9:6-7; 11:1-16).

TWO RESURRECTIONS

The Bible mentions two future resurrections for mankind. The *"First Resurrection"* (Rev. 20:5) is a resurrection of the Righteous, which will take place *before* the Millennium. It will include all of the different companies of the redeemed, those saved from each Dispensation. The Tribulation Saints will be the last company resurrected and translated. All of these will have a part in the First Resurrection, which is the resurrection of the living Saints who will Reign with Christ during the thousand years.

"I saw Thrones, and they sat upon them, and judgment was given unto them: and I saw the souls of them that were beheaded for the witness of Jesus, and for the Word of God, and which had not worshipped the Beast, neither his image, neither had received his mark upon their foreheads, or in their hands; AND THEY LIVED AND REIGNED WITH CHRIST A THOUSAND YEARS. But the rest of the dead lived not again until the thousand years were finished. This is the FIRST RESURRECTION. Blessed and Holy is he who has part in the FIRST RESURRECTION: on such the SECOND DEATH has no power, but they shall be Priests of God and of Christ, and shall reign with Him a THOUSAND YEARS" (Rev. 20:4-6).

The wicked dead will have no part in the First Resurrection, for they will not be resurrected until *after* the Millennium (Rev. 20:5). This is the Second Resurrection, which will include all of the wicked dead from each Dispensation, including from the Millennium. Their soul will remain in Hell until the end of the Millennium, when they will be resurrected to stand before the Great White Throne Judgment (Rev. 20:11-15):

"The SEA GAVE UP THE DEAD which were in it; and DEATH AND HELL DELIVERED UP THE DEAD which were in them: AND THEY WERE JUDGED EVERY MAN ACCORDING TO THEIR WORKS" (Rev. 20:13).

Those who have a part in the First Resurrection will be pronounced *"Blessed and Holy,"* but those who have a part in the Second Resurrection will have their part in the *"Lake of Fire"* (Rev. 20:15; 21:8).

GOVERNMENT OF THE MILLENNIAL KINGDOM

The Millennial Kingdom will be just as literal as any other previous earthly kingdom has been. God will set up a theocratic government reigning through Christ (Rev. 11:15; 20:1-10), through David, the king of Israel (Jer. 30:9; Ezek. 34:24; 37:24-28; Hos. 3:4-5), and through the Apostles and all the Saints from each Dispensation (Ps. 149:5-9; Dan. 7:18-27; Mat. 19:28; I Cor. 4:8; 6:2; II Tim. 2:12; Rev. 1:6; 2:26-27; 5:9-10; 20:4-6). The Saints will be given responsibility and rewards in rulership according to their spiritual commitment and stewardship during their natural lifetime. They will be judged according to the deeds done in the body (I Cor. 3:13-15; II Cor. 5:10), as discussed in the last Chapter.

Jerusalem will be the center of government for the kingdom, for the city will be rebuilt and restored to a greater glory than ever before. Jerusalem, as the world capital, will be the center of political, economic, and spiritual activity forever (I Chron. 23:25; II Chron. 33:4-7; Isa. 2:2-4; Jer. 17:25; Joel 3:20; Zech. 8:3-23; 14:1-21):

"It shall come to pass IN THE LAST DAYS, that the mountain of the LORD'S HOUSE SHALL BE ESTABLISHED IN THE TOP OF THE MOUNTAINS, and shall be exalted above the hills; and ALL NATIONS SHALL FLOW UNTO IT. And many people shall go and say, Come ye, and let us go up to the mountain of the LORD, to the House of the God of Jacob; and He will teach us of His Ways, and we will walk in His Paths: FOR OUT OF ZION SHALL GO FORTH THE LAW, and the Word of the LORD from JERUSALEM" (Isa. 2:2-3).

LAWS OF THE KINGDOM

The Millennial Kingdom will have various laws and regulations as in each of the preceding Dispensations. Man will have laws, serving as guidelines, that he will be expected to keep in all of Eternity, as well as during the Millennium. The Kingdom will be an earthly one with earthly subjects, and *some* hearts will rebel to an extent against the Rule of Christ. These will be people who have survived the Great Tribulation and who belong to the sheep nations; these will be permitted to enter the Millennium (Mat. 25:31-34).

That there will be sinners in the Millennial Kingdom is clear from I Corinthians 15:24-28; Isaiah 11:3-5; 65:20; Revelation 20:7-10; *et al*:

"WITH RIGHTEOUSNESS SHALL HE (the Branch) *JUDGE the poor; AND REPROVE with equity for the meek of the Earth: and he shall smite the Earth with the rod of His Mouth, and with the breath of His Lips shall he slay THE WICKED"* (Isa. 11:4).

"There shall be no more thence an infant of days, nor an old man who has not filled his days: for the child shall die an hundred years old; but the SINNER being an hundred years old shall be accursed" (Isa. 65:20).

These people will relate to the outward laws and government, but their heart will not be transformed. If a person commits any sin worthy of death, he will be executed (Isa. 11:3-5; 65:20).

There will be laws to govern and to keep order, and swift action will be executed for refusal to follow the Rules and Law of God. There will be no more lengthy court proceedings, appeals, and injustice, for God Himself will be the final Judge. Those who have been truly Born-Again and fully committed to the Lord, and have fellowship with God during the thousand years, certainly will not rebel against the Lord.

The laws of the Millennial Kingdom will include those originally given to Israel as an eternal standard of Holiness (Isa. 2:2-4; Mic. 4:1-2; Ezek. 40:1 through 48:35) and the laws of the New Covenant given by Christ. The terms of the Gospel will apply to every man, while some of the laws will apply only to Israel in her land. Certain of the feasts of Israel will be required upon all nations; for if they disobey, their lands will not receive rain (Zech. 14:16-21). We may be sure that God clearly will make known all of the laws that He will enforce during this time.

NATIONS OF THE EARTH

During this time nations as we know them today will continue to exist in many cases. Perhaps most of the Gentile nations will live in much the same places as they do now, with the exception of those who live in lands promised to Israel. This will include all of the land from the Mediterranean Sea on the west to the Euphrates River on the east, taking in all of the Arabian Peninsula and the wilderness countries, south and east of Palestine (Gen. 15:14-18; 17:6-19; Ezek. 47:13-23). There will be divisions in the Promised Land, running in wide strips east and west, with each of the Twelve Tribes of Israel receiving a possession (Ezek. 48:1-35).

MILLENNIAL TEMPLE

There will be a Millennial Temple for the Jews. This Temple, with its enclosure called *"the sanctuary,"* will be one mile square (Ezek. 45:1-4). This will not be the Temple built in the days before the Second Coming of Christ, where the Antichrist will rule for the last half of the Great Tribulation (Mat. 24:15-22; II Thess. 2:4). That Temple will be destroyed when Christ returns. This Millennial Temple will be built by Christ Himself when He comes back to Earth to set up His earthly Kingdom. It will be Christ's earthly Throne forever (Ezek. 43:7):

"Behold the Man Whose Name is The BRANCH; and He shall grow up out of His place, and He shall build THE TEMPLE OF THE LORD: Even He shall build THE TEMPLE OF THE LORD; and He shall bear the glory, and shall sit and rule upon His Throne; and He shall be a Priest upon His Throne: and the counsel of peace shall be . . . in THE TEMPLE OF THE LORD" (Zech. 6:12-14).

PRIESTS OF THE TEMPLE

There will be priests in this Temple as there were in the first Temple. Descendants of Levi will be involved in service, and the sons of Zadok who have been true to the house of David will do some of the most Holy work (II Sam. 8:17; 15:24; 20:25; I Ki. 1:39; Ezek. 43:19-27; 44:9-31). It is indicated that the priesthood of Moses and of his law is an *eternal* one (Ex. 29:9; 40:15; Num. 25:11-13; I Chron. 23:13):

"The Holy portion of the land shall be for the PRIESTS THE MIN-ISTERS OF THE SANCTUARY, which shall come near to minister unto the LORD: and it shall be a place for their houses, and an Holy place for the Sanctuary" (Ezek. 45:4).

This, however, is not in conflict with Hebrews 7:11-28, for there will be a change in the approach to Salvation and mediation with God, although the basic requirements will exist. Christ is our Passover, sacrificed once and forever, as contrasted to the regular offerings and sacrifices. The offerings of the priesthood will be not for Salvation, but for a memorial and object lesson to show the people what *already* has been accomplished through Christ. These offerings will be as Communion is today: a memorial regarding what Jesus did in His Redemptive Work at Calvary.

In Ezekiel, Chpts. 43-46 nearly all of the feasts that were observed by the Jews are mentioned as being celebrated in the Millennial Kingdom. These offerings and feasts, new moons and Sabbaths, and various ordinances and activities will be observed during the Millennium and in the New Earth forever (Isa. 66:22-24; Ezek. 44:5; 45:17; 46:1-3).

FLOWING RIVER

Flowing out from the Millennial Temple will be a literal river. It will flow eastward and from the south side of the Altar, and then will turn to go southward through Jerusalem, dividing the city, with half of the river flowing westward into the Mediterranean Sea and the other half flowing into the Dead Sea. The Dead Sea will be healed, so that once again life will exist in it, with multitudes of fish and sea life (Ezek. 47:1-12; Zech. 14:8):

"Afterward He brought me again unto the door of the house; and, behold, WATERS ISSUED OUT from under the threshold of the house eastward . . . and IT WAS A RIVER that I could not pass over: for the waters were risen, waters to swim in, A RIVER THAT COULD NOT BE PASSED OVER" (Ezek. 47:1-5).

A great earthquake will take place at the Second Coming when Christ sets His Foot on the Mount of Olives, causing a significant change for the whole country (Zech. 14:4-5). The Dead Sea will be provided an outlet to purify its stagnant waters, having been raised so that it can give life and sustenance:

"His feet shall stand in that day upon the Mount of Olives, which is before Jerusalem on the east, and THE MOUNT OF OLIVES SHALL CLEAVE IN THE MIDST THEREOF toward the east and toward the west, and there shall be a very great valley; and HALF OF THE MOUNTAIN SHALL REMOVE TOWARD THE NORTH, AND HALF OF IT TOWARD THE SOUTH. And you shall flee . . . like as you fled from before the EARTHQUAKE in the days of Uzziah king of Judah: and the LORD my God shall come, and all the Saints with you" (Zech. 14:4-5).

SPIRITUAL CONDITIONS OF THE MILLENNIUM

Marvelous spiritual conditions will exist during the Millennium. The Spirit of God already has been outpoured in a great and mighty way, beginning to a degree with the Day of Pentecost and experiencing great fulfillment in these latter days; but this will be completed fully and fulfilled in the Millennium and continuing on forever (Joel 2:28-32; Ezek. 36:25-27; Acts 2:1-16, 38-39). During the Millennium there will be prosperity for all nations and glorious peace and universal religious activities (Dan. 7:13-14, 18-27; Rev. 11:15; 20:1 through 21:13).

During this time universal knowledge also will abound (Isa. 11:9; Hab. 2:14; Zech. 8:22-23). Great insight and understanding will exist, and there will be real freedom for the expansion and assimilation of knowledge and understanding:

"The Earth shall be FILLED WITH THE KNOWLEDGE of the Glory OF THE LORD, as the waters cover the sea" (Hab. 2:14).

There also will be missionaries during the Millennium. The Jewish people will become great missionaries of the Gospel and priests of the Law during this age and forever (Isa. 2:2-4; 40:9; 52:7; 61:6; 66:18-21; Zech. 8:23):

"Yea, many people and strong nations shall come to seek the LORD of Hosts in Jerusalem, and to pray before the LORD. Thus saith the

LORD of Hosts; IN THOSE DAYS IT SHALL COME TO PASS, THAT TEN MEN shall take hold out of all languages of the nations, even SHALL TAKE HOLD OF THE SKIRT OF HIM WHO IS A JEW, saying, We will go with you: FOR WE HAVE HEARD THAT GOD IS WITH YOU" (Zech. 8:22-23).

The Promise was given to Abraham that his seed would be a blessing to all nations. And one way in which they will bless the world is that they will carry out a missionary program such as we have today:

"HOW BEAUTIFUL UPON THE MOUNTAINS ARE THE FEET OF HIM WHO BRINGS GOOD TIDINGS, Who publishes peace; Who brings good tidings of good, Who publishes Salvation; Who says unto Zion, YOUR GOD REIGNS! Your watchmen shall lift up the voice; with the voice together shall they sing: for they shall see eye to eye, when the LORD shall bring again Zion. Break forth into joy, sing together, you waste places of Jerusalem: for the LORD has comforted His People, He has redeemed Jerusalem. The LORD has made bare His Holy Arm in the eyes of all the nations; and ALL THE ENDS OF THE EARTH SHALL SEE THE SALVATION OF OUR GOD" (Isa. 52:7-10).

There will be people during the Millennium who have not made a personal commitment to Christ and who have not had a true Born-Again experience that will come to know Him. There will be those repenting and accepting Christ as today, and Salvation will be for all, but they will need to make that personal commitment (Joel 2:32; Acts 2:16-21; Isa. 2:2-4; 11:9; 52:7):

"It shall come to pass, that whosoever shall call on the Name of the Lord shall be saved" (Acts 2:21).

In addition to all these blessings, there will be Divine Healing for all (Isa. 32:1-5; 33:24; 35:3-6; 53:5), for Christ will be the Great Physician:

"STRENGTHEN YE THE WEAK HANDS, AND CONFIRM THE FEEBLE KNEES. Say to them who are of a fearful heart, Be strong, fear not: behold, your God will come with vengeance, even God with a recompence; He will come and save you. THEN THE EYES OF THE BLIND SHALL BE OPENED, and THE EARS OF THE DEAF SHALL BE UNSTOPPED. THEN SHALL THE LAME MAN LEAP as an hart, and THE TONGUE OF THE DUMB SING: for in the wilderness shall waters break out, and streams in the desert" (Isa. 35:3-6).

LIVING CONDITIONS OF THE MILLENNIUM

Living conditions during the Millennium will be most wonderful. There will be no tempter, as Satan will be bound! There will be universal peace (Isa. 2:4; 9:6-7; Mic. 4:3-4). Swords will not be used for war, but rather they will be implemented for constructive use:

"He shall judge among many people, and rebuke strong nations afar off; and THEY SHALL BEAT THEIR SWORDS INTO PLOW-SHARES, AND THEIR SPEARS INTO PRUNINGHOOKS: nation shall not lift up a sword against nation, NEITHER SHALL THEY LEARN WAR ANYMORE. But they shall sit every man under his vine and under his fig tree; and none shall make them afraid: for the Mouth of the LORD of Hosts has spoken it" (Mic. 4:3-4).

There will be no harboring of prejudices and national ills. Spiritual revivals will break out in every land; and as people turn to God, they will be united in serving Christ. Attention will not be focused on wars, recessions, and depressions. People will live in full satisfaction with peace and prosperity, knowing the Goodness and Blessings of God in His wonderful Reign:

"FOR FROM THE RISING OF THE SUN EVEN UNTO THE GOING DOWN OF THE SAME MY NAME SHALL BE GREAT AMONG THE GENTILES; and in every place incense shall be offered unto My Name, and a pure offering: for MY NAME SHALL BE GREAT AMONG THE HEATHEN, saith the LORD of Hosts" (Mal. 1:11).

There will be neither need nor want, as man feeds on universal prosperity (Isa. 65:24; Mic. 4:4-5). Unemployment and poverty will cease to be because there will not be great amounts of money spent on evils as in our present day. Tithing was practiced before the Law (Gen. 14:20; 28:22), as well as under the Law (Lev. 27:30-33), and tithing also has been employed since the Law (Mat. 23:23; I Cor. 9:7-18; 16:1-3). This type of system will supply ample provisions for everyone. Since there will be no need for special taxes, great assistance will be given to promoting the presentation of the Gospel.

LONGEVITY DURING MILLENNIUM

During this time human life will be prolonged (Isa. 65:20; Zech. 8:4). The glorified Saints ruling with Christ at this time, of course, will be immortal, but natural people will continue to live. They will be able to live a thousand years; and if they do not ally with Satan and rebel against God at the end, they will live forever and ever.

Man was made to live a long time. Adam lived 900 years and Methusaleh lived 969 years. Enoch lived 365 years on Earth, and has lived for over 5,000 years in Heaven in his natural body! The human body virtually replenishes itself every seven years and should live on indefinitely, and will during this time.

There will be an increase of light (Isa. 30:26; 60:18-22) to the extent that it will be increased seven times, and the light of the moon will be as the light of the sun today:

"Moreover the LIGHT OF THE MOON SHALL BE AS THE LIGHT OF THE SUN, and THE LIGHT OF THE SUN SHALL BE SEVENFOLD, as the light of seven days, in the day that the LORD binds up the breach of His People, and heals the stroke of their wound" (Isa. 30:26).

"The sun shall be no more your light by day; neither for brightness shall the moon give light unto you: but the LORD shall be unto you AN EVERLASTING LIGHT, and your God your glory" (Isa. 60:19).

Light has healing and restorative powers, and this also may relate to man's longevity.

TEST OF THIS DISPENSATION

Changes will be evidenced in the animal kingdom (Isa. 11:6-8; 65:17-25; Rom. 8:18-23). Their very nature will be transformed. No longer will they be fierce; they will not kill; and they will not be poisonous.

"THE WOLF ALSO SHALL DWELL WITH THE LAMB, and THE LEOPARD SHALL LIE DOWN WITH THE KID; and THE CALF AND THE YOUNG LION AND THE FATLING TOGETHER; and A LITTLE CHILD SHALL LEAD THEM. And THE COW AND THE BEAR SHALL FEED; THEIR YOUNG ONES SHALL LIE DOWN TOGETHER: and THE LION SHALL EAT STRAW LIKE THE OX. AND THE SUCK-LING CHILD SHALL PLAY ON THE HOLE OF THE ASP, and THE WEANED CHILD SHALL PUT HIS HAND ON THE COCKATRICE' DEN. THEY SHALL NOT HURT NOR DESTROY IN ALL MY HOLY MOUNTAIN: for the Earth shall be full of the Knowledge of the LORD, as the waters cover the sea" (Isa. 11:6-9).

The Earth will be restored to the wonderful beauty of its original condition (Isa. 35:1-10; 55:12-13; Ezek. 36:8-12; Joel 2:18-27; 3:17-21; Amos 9:13-15; Rom. 8:18-23).

During this administration man will face the test of obedience to the laws of Divine Government and to Christ and the test of molding his character in harmony with God (Rev. 5:10; 11:15; 20:1-10).

LOOSING OF SATAN AFTER MILLENNIUM

After the thousand years are fulfilled, Satan will be loosed out of his prison and will attempt to deceive the nations:

"When the thousand years are expired, SATAN SHALL BE LOOSED OUT OF HIS PRISON, And shall go out to deceive the nations which are in the four quarters of the Earth, GOG AND MAGOG, to gather

them together to battle: the number of whom is as the sand of the sea. And they went up on the breadth of the Earth, and compassed the camp of the Saints about, and the beloved city: AND FIRE CAME DOWN FROM GOD OUT OF HEAVEN, AND DEVOURED THEM. AND THE DEVIL WHO DECEIVED THEM WAS CAST INTO THE LAKE OF FIRE AND BRIMSTONE, where the Beast and the False Prophet are, AND SHALL BE TORMENTED DAY AND NIGHT FOREVER AND EVER" (Rev. 20:7-10).

The Greek word for *"deceive"* used in this passage is *planao*, which means *"to cause to wander or to go astray."* It relates to doctrinal error and deceit, and this is what Satan will do as he tries to deceive men.

During the Millennium millions of natural people on Earth will have had that period of time in which to accept Christ as Savior and truly submit to God. Having retained their fallen Adamic nature, they will be subject in various ways to the influence of Satan when he is loosed. Satan will recruit followers that will seek to help him overthrow the Kingdom of God, and he will lead them against the Saints at Jerusalem.

The expression *"Gog and Magog"* (Rev. 20:8) relates to the Gentiles who rebel at this time, and is not to be confused with the *"Gog"* and *"Magog"* mentioned in Ezekiel, Chpts. 38-39. The destruction of these groups from the east and west will occur after the Millennium. As they come against the Kingdom and seek to take the city, fire will descend from God and devour them. Satan, the great deceiver, will be cast, finally, into the Lake of Fire where the Beast and the False Prophet will have been confined since the Battle of Armageddon (which will immediately precede the Millennium).

GREAT WHITE THRONE JUDGMENT

Following this will be the Great White Throne Judgment:

"I saw A GREAT WHITE THRONE, and Him Who sat on it, from Whose Face the Earth and the Heaven fled away; and there was found no place for them. And I saw the DEAD, SMALL AND GREAT, STAND BEFORE GOD; and the BOOKS WERE OPENED: and another Book was opened, which is the Book of Life: and THE DEAD WERE JUDGED OUT OF THOSE THINGS WHICH WERE WRITTEN IN THE BOOKS, ACCORDING TO THEIR WORKS. And the sea gave up the dead which were in it; and death and Hell delivered up the dead which were in them: and they were JUDGED EVERY MAN ACCORDING TO THEIR WORKS. And death and Hell were cast into the Lake of Fire. This is the second death. AND WHOSOEVER WAS NOT

FOUND WRITTEN IN THE BOOK OF LIFE WAS CAST INTO THE LAKE OF FIRE" (Rev. 20:11-15).

This passage states that Heaven and Earth fled from His *"Face."* The Greek word for *"Face"* is *prosopon*, which means *"the countenance, aspect, appearance, surface, front view, outward appearance, face, and person."* It indicates that God has an outward person and a real body. In other places in the New Testament this same word has reference to a bodily presence and its actual appearance.

There are many things that need to be observed concerning the Great White Throne Judgment. God is the Judge (Heb. 12:23-29; 13:4; Rev. 6:10; Acts 17:30-31), as well as Christ (Jn. 5:19-27; Acts 10:42; 17:30-31; II Tim. 4:8; Rev. 19:11). Those judged at this time will be the wicked people of the entire human race (Acts 17:31; Rom. 3:6). However, this will not include the Beast, the False Prophet, and the goat nations, for their sentence already will have been pronounced 1,000 years earlier, and that Judgment need not be repeated (Mat. 13:30, 39-43, 49-50; 24:51; 25:30, 41, 46; Rev. 14:9-11; 20:10).

This Judgment will come to pass after the Millennium, and after Satan has been cast into the Lake of Fire. It will be a specific *"Day of Judgment"* and will be set at a definite time (Mat. 10:15; 11:24; 12:36; Acts 17:31; II Pet. 2:4; Jude, Vss. 6-7). This Judgment will take place before the Throne of God.

At this time the Throne will be still in Heaven, for it will not come to Earth until after the Earth has been renovated by fire, which, it seems, will take place immediately after this Judgment (II Pet. 3:7). All the secrets of men (Rom. 2:16), their works, their thoughts, and all their actions will be judged (I Tim. 5:24; I Pet. 1:17; Rev. 20:12-13).

Before man is condemned and punished, he will stand trial and understand clearly the reason for his Judgment. There will be no excuse for, or criticism of, the sentence. His conscience will divulge his sins (Rom. 2:12-16). The law will be clear, and the Gospel will be a significant basis for the Judgment (Rom. 2:12-16; Jn. 12:47-48; Rev. 20:11-15). The Book of Life will be opened, and every man's works will be revealed.

BOOK OF LIFE

There are many references to the Book of Life in the Word of God (Ex. 32:23, 33; Dan. 12:1; Lk. 10:20; Phil. 4:3; Rev. 3:5; 13:8; 17:8; 20:12-15; 21:27; 22:19). The Book of Life has in it the names of those who have entered into life and who are committed to the Lord. Basically the reference to *"Books"* in Revelation 20:12 relates to the Word of God, which will judge men.

The dead here do no include Angels, but mortals who have died and gone to Hell, which we know to be different from the Lake of Fire, or eternal Hell, because *"death and Hell were cast into the Lake of Fire. This is the second death"* (Rev. 20:14). Hades is the present place of confinement for the souls of the wicked, and there they are conscious and in torment until the Resurrection (Lk. 16:19-31).

Hell will have degrees of punishment and torment and fire, just as Heaven will have degrees of rewards and bliss and comfort for those that are good and faithful. The degrees of punishment conceivably would come primarily through the torment of man's inner conscience and awareness of evil deeds committed, together with the realization of failures made and the refusals to commit their lives to Christ.

Punishment is eternal. Those who receive life have everlasting life, and the same Greek word *aionion*, which means *"forever,"* is applied also to the matter of punishment (Mat. 25:41-46; Mk. 9:43-47; Lk. 12:5; Heb. 6:2; 10:26-31; Rev. 14:9-11; 19:20; 20:10-15; 21:8).

HEAVENS AND EARTH RENOVATED

It is stated in Revelation 21:1 that following the Great White Throne Judgment, the heavens and the Earth will pass away. The general conception is that the present Heaven and Earth will be completely annihilated, or cease to exist, but this is not the case. The renovation of the Earth will be timed after the Millennium and the casting of Satan into the Lake of Fire, and the Great White Throne Judgment. The Throne will come down to the New Earth with the Holy City and be with men forever.

The present Heaven and Earth will not cease to exist or pass away completely. Many readers receive that impression from II Peter 3:10-13; Revelation 20:11; 21:1; but a more careful observation of these passages will reflect some other views:

"The Day of the Lord will come as a thief in the night; in the which THE HEAVENS SHALL PASS AWAY with a great noise, and THE ELEMENTS SHALL MELT WITH FERVENT HEAT, the Earth also and the works that are therein SHALL BE BURNED UP. Seeing then that all these things SHALL BE DISSOLVED, what manner of persons ought ye to be in all Holy conversation and Godliness, Looking for and hasting unto THE COMING OF THE DAY OF GOD, wherein the heavens being on fire shall be dissolved, and the elements shall melt with fervent heat? Nevertheless we, according to His Promise, look for NEW HEAVENS AND A NEW EARTH, wherein dwelleth Righteousness" (II Pet. 3:10-13).

"I saw a Great White Throne, and Him Who sat on it, from Whose Face THE EARTH AND THE HEAVEN FLED AWAY; and there was found no place for them" (Rev. 20:11).

"I saw A NEW HEAVEN AND A NEW EARTH: for the FIRST HEAVEN AND THE FIRST EARTH WERE PASSED AWAY; and there was no more sea" (Rev. 21:1).

According to II Peter 3:10-13, the present Heaven and Earth will not be annihilated. The fire does not destroy them. Fire changes something from one state to another, and Peter was showing that there simply will be a renovation of the Earth by fire, that the Earth will not be obliterated totally anymore than it was with the destruction of the world by water in the beginning.

The word in the Greek that is translated *"pass away"* is *parerchomai* and means *"to go by, or away from,"* in the sense of passing from one condition to another. It never is used to indicate a ceasing of existence. There are many instances where this is used, and in at least 75 instances it means such things as the passing of time (Mat. 7:28; 9:10; 11:1; 13:53) and events (Mat. 24:6; Lk. 21:7; Jn. 14:29).

Parerchomai is the word used in reference to the infallibility of God's Word, showing that it is easier for a change in Heaven and Earth than it is for God's Word to fail (Mat. 5:18; 24:34-35; Mk. 13:31; Lk. 16:17). It also is used in reference to God's People passing by certain places (Mk. 6:48; Lk. 18:37), and in Luke 12:37 and 17:7 it refers to the coming of an individual. There are numerous other examples, but not one of them is used with reference to the passing out of existence; so it is felt that II Peter 3:10 clearly means passing from one condition to another, as does Hebrews 1:12; 12:27-28.

Second Peter 3:10 also speaks of the elements melting with fervent heat. The Greek word for *"elements"* is *stoicheion*, meaning *"something orderly in arrangement, element, principle, or rudiment."* It has to do with foundation principles regarding the questions that are involved. In Galatians 4:3, 9; Colossians 2:8, 20; II Pet. 2:10, 12 the word embraces the principles of sin and the present world system. It embodies sinful nature, disease, bad spirits, and corruption, and includes a part of the present bondage and corruption that must be destroyed (Rom. 8:18-25).

The word that is translated *"melt"* is *luo*, meaning *"to loose, put off, unbind, untie, or set free."* It is translated this way in several scriptures (Mat. 21:2; Lk. 19:30, 33; Jn. 1:27; 11:44; Acts 7:33) and is rendered *"dissolved"* in II Peter 3:11-12. It seems these passages establish that the present heavens and Earth will be renovated by being loosed from bondage and that they will be changed into a new state (Rom. 8:21-23).

The Scriptures indicate that only those things that need to be renovated will be burned. Many things will remain as they are now, such as mankind and animals. Romans 8:18-25 speaks of the whole Creation of God at the time of Adam as remaining forever, and further reveals their deliverance from the present bondage to the state of glorious liberty and the manifestation of the sons of God.

It is also apparent from Hebrews 12:26-28 that some things will be destroyed while other things will *"remain"* and that there will be a kingdom received that *"cannot be moved."*

Another statement indicating change rather than annihilation is Hebrews 1:10-12. God has the interest of His creatures at heart, and these will not be totally destroyed or annihilated. Fire certainly will consume wicked and rebellious things out of the camp of the Saints, but there are many expressions that there are those things ordained by God that will remain forever.

RESULT OF MILLENNIUM

Second Corinthians 5:17 states that *"old things are passed away"* and *"all things are become new"* for the Christian. Yet, we know that there are many basic physical aspects of an individual that are essentially the same. This is the same idea as for the renewal of the Heaven and the Earth. Even as the Believer *"pass*(s) *from death unto life"* (Jn. 5:24) at the new birth, this old world also will be transformed into a beautiful condition. God will restore the Earth to a perfected state, even as it was in the beginning before Lucifer rebelled or Adam fell from God's favor.

We shall discuss further the New Heavens and the New Earth in the next chapter.

God's Plan For The Ages

PART
THREE

THE ETERNAL
FUTURE

Chapter 12

The New Heavens And The New Earth — The Ages To Come

CHAPTER TWELVE

THE NEW HEAVENS AND
THE NEW EARTH —
THE AGES TO COME

(Isa. 65:17; 66:22-24; II Pet. 3:13; Rev., Chpts. 21-22)

DESCRIPTION BY JOHN THE REVELATOR

John the Revelator beautifully described the beginning of the eternal perfect state:

"I saw a NEW HEAVEN AND A NEW EARTH: for the first Heaven and the first Earth were passed away; and there was no more sea. And I John saw the Holy City, New Jerusalem, coming down from God out of Heaven, prepared as a bride adorned for her husband. And I heard a great Voice out of Heaven saying, Behold, the Tabernacle of God is with men, and He will dwell with them, and they shall be His People, and God Himself shall be with them, and be their God. And God shall wipe away all tears from their eyes; and there shall be no more death, neither sorrow, nor crying, neither shall there be any more pain; for the former things are passed away" (Rev. 21:1-4).

The New heavens and the New Earth will be the great climax to the eternal Plan of God. Since the beginning God has determined to dwell with His creation in a perfect environment, free from sin, sickness, sorrow, and pain! He has longed to walk with man *"in the cool of the day"* (Gen. 3:8), as He did in the Garden of Eden, and have eternal fellowship with him. This will become a wonderful reality in the New Earth! With the extinction of the curse and its effect upon the creation, man is truly yet to enjoy *"Heaven on Earth!"*

JERUSALEM AN ETERNAL CITY

Jerusalem will be an eternal possession of the New Earth, and will be a place of rejoicing, and her people will be full of joy (II Chron. 33:4; Jer. 17:25; Ezek. 43:7):

"In JERUSALEM shall My Name be FOREVER" (II Chron. 33:4).
"And THIS CITY shall remain FOR EVER" (Jer. 17:25).

In the eternal city of Jerusalem there will be only happiness, for every tear will be eternally wiped away (Rev. 21:4). Israel is assured that she will be an eternal earthly people (Isa. 66:22-24). There is a promise that Israel's seed and name will remain forever. By the same token, there will be the new moons and Sabbaths, and the worship of *"all flesh"* before God forever:

"For as the New Heaven and the New Earth . . . shall remain before Me . . . SO SHALL YOUR SEED AND YOUR NAME REMAIN" (Isa. 66:22-24).

"I will dwell in the midst of the Children of Israel FOREVER" (Ezek. 43:7).

PLACE OF RIGHTEOUSNESS

Only Righteousness will dwell in the new state, as declared in II Peter 3:10-13. There will be no more temptation, no more sin, and no more horrible consequences of sin! Satan no longer will be *"the prince of this world"* (Jn. 12:31; 14:30; 16:11), for God shall reign supreme forever and ever!

The New Earth no longer will contain the large oceans now covering three-fourths of the Earth, for *"there* (will be) *no more sea"* (Rev. 21:1). However, there will be rivers and lakes and smaller seas forever. There also will be changes in the land masses. Without the oceans there will not be islands, but some seas will continue to exist eternally (Jer. 5:22; 31:35; Ps. 146:6):

"(He has) placed the sand for THE BOUND OF THE SEA BY A PERPETUAL DECREE, THAT IT CANNOT PASS IT: and though the waves thereof toss themselves, yet can they not prevail; though they roar, yet can they not pass over it?" (Jer. 5:22).

TABERNACLE OF GOD

"The Tabernacle of God (will be) *with men"* (Rev. 21:3). It is a literal tabernacle that will come down from God with the New Jerusalem to remain upon the Earth. That it will be *"with men"* must refer to the natural men on Earth, for the Glorified Saints already will have been with God for 1,000 years.

God will come down to these earthly people who have lived through the Millennium without rebelling against the Kingdom as did those who rebelled at the end of the Millennium under the leadership of Satan. These people will not become Glorified, but will remain in a natural state. However, they will be imperishable as God intended man to be when He created him.

God's eternal Purpose was not changed because of the fall of man, and once again the human race will continue to live as originally intended. God will dwell, or tabernacle among men, in the midst of them (Jn. 1:14; Rev. 7:15; 12:12; 13:6). God the Father Himself will be visible to them and will be *Immanuel* — GOD WITH US (Mat. 1:23; Ps. 68:16-18; Isa. 7:14; Zech. 2:10-11):

"Sing and rejoice, O daughter of Zion: for, lo, I come, and I WILL DWELL IN THE MIDST OF YOU, saith the LORD. And many nations shall be joined to the LORD in that day, and shall be My People: and I will dwell in the midst of you, and you shall know that the LORD of Hosts has sent Me unto you. And the LORD shall inherit Judah His portion in the Holy Land, and shall choose Jerusalem again" (Zech. 2:10-12).

NO MORE SORROW, CRYING, OR PAIN

God also will *"wipe away tears from off all faces"* (Isa. 25:8). The things that cause sorrow and regret will be removed forever. A most marvelous and glorious statement is made:

"God shall wipe away all tears from their eyes; and there shall be NO MORE death, neither SORROW, nor CRYING, neither shall there be any more PAIN: for the former things are passed away" (Rev. 21:4).

All these things will be removed; the sin and the curse will be taken away from the human race to be no more. The end result of sin is death (Rom. 6:23). The devil has caused both death and destruction, but the natural man of the future Kingdom on Earth will experience the fulfillment of Exodus 32:13; Psalms 25:13; 37:9-11; 69:36; 82:8; Isaiah 60:1-22.

Conditions will be conducive only to perfection and for good in the New Earth, and the race will be perpetuated without the difficulties caused by the Devil. However, while human beings will not die in the New Earth, animals will be sacrificed, thus meaning that they will continue to die.

ALL THINGS MADE NEW

"Behold, I make all things new" (Rev. 21:5). The word for *"new"* here is the same as in *"I saw a New Heaven and a New Earth"* (Rev. 21:1) and indicates that things will be *not destroyed*, but rather *renewed*. The Promise also is given:

"I will give unto him that is athirst of the fountain of the Water of Life freely. HE WHO OVERCOMES SHALL INHERIT ALL THINGS; and I will be his God, and he shall be My son" (Rev. 21:6-7).

At the same time, on the other hand, Judgment upon the wicked equally is assured:

"The FEARFUL, and UNBELIEVING, and the ABOMINABLE, and MURDERERS, and WHOREMONGERS, and SORCERERS, and IDOLATERS, and ALL LIARS, shall have their part in the LAKE which burns with FIRE AND BRIMSTONE: which is the second death" (Rev. 21:8).

NO MORE DEATH

Natural people will exist in the New Earth from generation to generation forever (Gen. 9:12; 13:15; 17:7, 19; Ex. 3:15; 12:14, 42; 27:21; 30:8, 21; 31:16; 40:15; Ps. 12:7; 45:17; 100:5; 146:10; Isa. 59:21).

There are three passages that speak of a *"thousand generations"* (Deut. 7:9; I Chron. 16:15; Ps. 105:8). This is a Hebrew expression meaning *"perpetual generations,"* and is stated thus in Genesis 9:12.

The priesthood of Aaron and his seed are referred to as being eternal (Ex. 29:9; 40:15; Num. 25:11-13; I Chron. 23:13).

Other things considered eternal are burning incense on the Altar (Ex. 30:8; II Chron. 2:4), Covenants (Gen. 9:16; Ex. 31:16; Num. 18:19; I Chron. 16:17; Jer. 32:40; Ezek. 37:26), and also the Sacrificial Offerings (Ezek. 46:1-24).

The land promised to Abraham was to be an eternal possession (Gen. 13:15; 17:6-8; 48:4; Ex. 32:13; Lev. 25:23, 30, 34; Deut. 4:40; Josh. 14:2, 9).

There are also other priestly activities, such as ceremonial cleansings (Ex. 30:17-21; Num. 19:20), new moons and Sabbaths (Ex. 31:16-17; II Chron. 2:4; Isa. 66:22-23), which are eternal.

There will be perpetual natural life for men and continuation of the animal kingdom (Gen. 9:9-17).

The natural seed of David and his throne and kingdom will be eternal and will be ruled by Christ forever (II Sam. 7:11-17; I Ki. 2:45; 9:3-5; I Chron. 17:7-14; II Chron. 13:5; Ps. 89:3-4; Isa. 9:6-7; Dan. 2:44-45; Mic. 4:7; Heb. 1:8; Rev. 11:15; 22:5).

In all of these references the translation is *"everlasting," "for ever,"* or *"perpetual,"* which denotes the Eternity of God. We take these words to be used in the eternal sense, as is clear from the passages themselves, and we are taking the scriptures on these matters *literally* since there is no contrary implication.

UNIVERSE INHABITED

God has created all things, and man, His highest Creation, is *"to have dominion over* (all) *the works of* (His) *Hands"* (Ps. 8:6). This includes the planets and the entire universe. It figures, then, that man's full possessive rights will give him access to this portion of God's Creation in the future restoration. As natural people continue to propagate, it will be at a slower rate. Nevertheless, over the eons there will be a substantial increase in the number of people. There will be no special problem for them to have space in which to exist. Without the oceans and with fuller utilization of space, this Earth can accommodate many times the present world population. Then, the other planets and the vast universe itself will be a part of man's domain also.

LITERAL CITY

John saw the Holy City, the New Jerusalem, prepared as a bride for her husband, coming down from God out of Heaven:

"I John saw the HOLY CITY, NEW JERUSALEM, coming down from God out of Heaven, prepared as a BRIDE ADORNED FOR HER HUSBAND. . . . And there came unto me one of the seven Angels . . . and talked with me, saying, Come hither, I will show you the bride, the LAMB'S WIFE. And he carried me away in the Spirit to a great and high mountain, and showed me that great city, the Holy Jerusalem, descending out of Heaven from God" (Rev. 21:2, 9-11).

References to this prove that it will be a literal city and that this is not symbolic of a group of people. It is known by several names, one of which is the New Jerusalem.

The word *"New"* here in the Greek is the same as the *"New"* in Revelation 21:1, speaking of the New Heaven and the New Earth. In this case, however, the city will not have been sinful or corrupt and will not need a renovation. So, the meaning here is that a freshness, or newness, in character will exist. All things in the eternal Presence of God are ever new and fresh, so here it is indicating a new freshness.

The fact that New Jerusalem was created in the beginning with the heavens and the Earth is reasonable since the Throne of God is located there, and it has been in existence since the heavens were created (Ps. 11:4; 93:2; 103:19; Isa. 6:1; 66:1; Rev. 4:2-10; 5:1-13; 7:9-17; 8:3; 22:1-3).

The word *"Jerusalem"* (used 810 times in the Bible) always is spoken of in a literal sense, and it is taken to be a literal Heavenly city here. It is called also the *"Holy City"* (Rev. 21:2; 22:19).

The word *"Holy"* never is used to deal with the character of a symbol, but always is used with something actual and real. This is a Holy and pure city, separated unto God.

The Holy City is also called *"the bride, the Lamb's wife"* (Rev. 21:2,

9). Many interpreters have taken this to be symbolic of the Church, but it clearly represents a literal city, and redeemed people inhabit it. The Scripture explicitly states here that John saw the bride, the Lamb's wife. He was being shown not the Church, but the Holy City, the New Jerusalem, descending down from God out of Heaven.

THE NEW JERUSALEM THE BRIDE OF CHRIST

What is the Bride of Christ?

The Bride of Christ is the Church, i.e., the *"Body of Christ."* The parable of the ten virgins portray the Bridegroom, Who is Christ, and the Bride, which is the Church (Mat. 25:1-13). John the Beloved wrote, *"He who has the Bride is the Bridegroom"* (Jn. 3:29). As is obvious here, Jesus is the Bridegroom and the Church, souls brought to Christ, constitute the "Bride." In Revelation, Chapter 21, the Scripture says, *"Come hither and I will show you the Bride, the Lamb's wife."* The Scripture then says, *"And he carried me away in the Spirit to a great and high mountain, and showed me that great city, the Holy Jerusalem, descending out of Heaven from God"* (Rev. 21:9-10).

The New Jerusalem will contain the Body of Christ, which is the Bride.

CITY PREPARED FOR THE SAINTS

Revelation 21:9-11 points to God as the source and origin of the New Jerusalem. Prepared by Him, it comes from Heaven to Earth to be the Eternal City, the Dwelling Place for God and His Heavenly People.

Notice that the city is *"prepared,"* which means it is made ready and provided for. Just as a bride is made ready for her husband, the New Jerusalem is made ready to be the abode of the Heavenly Saints, that the Tabernacle of God may be located among earthly men forever:

"The Tabernacle of God is WITH MEN, and He will dwell WITH THEM, and they shall be His People, and God Himself shall be WITH THEM, and be their God" (Rev. 21:3).

Jesus declared in John 14:1-4 that He was going to *"prepare"* a place for the Saints and that it would be made up of *"many mansions,"* which means *"places of residence, or abode"*:

"Let not your heart be troubled: you believe in God, believe also in me. IN MY FATHER'S HOUSE ARE MANY MANSIONS: if it were not so, I would have told you. I GO TO PREPARE A PLACE FOR YOU. And if I go and prepare a place for you, I will come again, and receive you unto Myself; that where I am, there you may be also" (Jn. 14:1-3).

The word *"prepare"* does not mean that Christ is waiting for materials, or that there is a building process going on. The *"place"* already has been created, and the idea is that Christ is making ready an abode for the People of God in a mansion that already exists, or is built, in the Father's House.

This is the usage of the word *"prepare"* in such passages as Matthew 20:23; 22:4; 25:34; 26:17; I Corinthians 2:9; II Timothy 2:21; Revelation 12:6; 16:12. The connotation in these references is not that of creativity or bringing into being, but that of making ready what already exists.

LOCATION OF THE NEW JERUSALEM

The eternal location of the New Jerusalem will be Earth itself. There are those who believe that the Holy City will be located in midair, but reference to the foundations of the city tends to discredit that theory. The descent from Heaven is unlikely to stop short of reaching Earth. Also, the fact that the nations of men on Earth will bring recognition, glory, and honor to it would certainly mean that the city will be located on Earth (Rev. 22:1-5):

"The NATIONS OF THEM WHICH ARE SAVED shall walk in the light of it: and THE KINGS OF THE EARTH do bring their glory and honour into it. And the gates of it shall be shut at all by day: for there shall be no night there. AND THEY SHALL BRING THE GLORY AND HONOUR OF THE NATIONS INTO IT" (Rev. 21:24-26).

CITY WHERE THE LAMB IS THE LIGHT

The Glory of God will be reflected throughout the city and is likened to the jasper stone (Rev. 21:11). A beautiful Light of radiant Glory will be seen throughout the New Jerusalem. The Bible tells us that the Lamb is the Light. Jesus Christ will be the Light of the Glory!

"The city had no need of the sun, neither of the moon, to shine in it: for THE GLORY OF GOD DID LIGHTEN IT, AND THE LAMB IS THE LIGHT THEREOF" (Rev. 21:23).

DIMENSIONS OF THE CITY

The wall of the city is *"great and high"* (Rev. 21:12-17) with three gates on each side of the four sides. Ezekiel's description of the eternal earthly city of Jerusalem, which is to be built ay the beginning of the Millennium (Ezek. 48:30-35), is actually a miniature of the Heavenly City.

The names if the Twelve Tribes of Israel will be inscribed on the Twelve gates in the wall. These names will appear also on the gates of the earthly Jerusalem (Ezek. 48:30-35). Angels will stand by the gates. The names of the Twelve Apostles will be inscribed on the foundations.

The Angel used a *"golden reed"* to measure the city, the gates, and the wall. A measuring reed of this kind is about 12-1/2 feet long (Ezek. 40:5; 41:8; 43:13):

"He who talked with me had a GOLDEN REED to measure the city, and the gates thereof, and the wall thereof. And the city lies FOUR-SQUARE, and THE LENGTH IS AS LARGE AS THE BREADTH: and he measured the city with the reed, twelve thousand furlongs. THE LENGTH AND THE BREADTH AND THE HEIGHT OF IT ARE EQUAL" (Rev. 21:15-16).

The New Jerusalem is built foursquare. The length, breadth, and height are equal, all being 12,000 furlongs or 1,500 miles. If this is understood to be a cube, it appears to be hollow inside, like an empty box, having about 3.375 billion cubic miles.

Or, it may be built like our modern skyscrapers, with layered stories. The description does not necessarily mean that it is an actual cube. It could conceivably taper in at the top and resemble a mountain peak, or pyramid, equal on all sides. In that case, it would be 4.054 million square miles, with mansions throughout, and it could accommodate billions of people.

The wall of the city is 144 cubits. Considering a cubit to be about 18 inches, the wall would be 215 feet high. If the structure were a cube, a wall that low would seem out of place. If the city towered upward from the base to 1,500 miles high, then the wall around the city apparently would be useful.

WALLS, GATES, AND STREETS

The building material if the wall is *"jasper"* (Rev. 21:18-21), and the city is *"pure gold, like unto clear glass."* The foundations of the wall are various precious stones: jasper, sapphire, chalcedony, emerald, sardonyx, sardius, chrysolyte, beryl, topaz, chrysoprasus, jacinth, and amethyst. Each stone used is precious, perfect, and priceless. The streets of the city are transparent gold; the gates, pearl.

TEMPLE

Revelation 21:22 states that John *"saw no Temple therein: for the Lord God Almighty and the Lamb are the Temple of it."*

Revelation 15:5 and 21:3, however, prove that there will be a literal Temple in the New Jerusalem. The idea conveyed here is that the personal Presence of God and the Lamb, in a real sense, will be a Sanctuary for God's People in the eternal state.

All previous worship on Earth has not had the personal Presence of God and the Lamb as Objects of worship. It is promised in Revelation 3:12 that the overcomer will have authority in the Temple of God and that there will be no more going out. Several other passages do refer to a Temple in the Holy City, a real place of God's continual Presence (Rev. 7:15; 11:19; 14:15, 17; 15:5, 8; 16:1, 17).

GLORY OF GOD

The light of the city will be greater than that of the sun, moon, and stars (Rev. 21:23, 25). Actually, there will be no need for these natural lights, for there will be no night there or darkness of any kind!

"There shall be no more curse: but the Throne of God and of the Lamb shall be in it; and His servants shall serve Him: And they shall see His Face; and His Name shall be in their foreheads. AND THERE SHALL BE NO NIGHT THERE; AND THEY NEED NO CANDLE, NEITHER LIGHT OF THE SUN; FOR THE LORD GOD GIVES THEM LIGHT: and they shall reign for ever and ever" (Rev. 22:3-5).

The brilliance of the Glory of God, Whose wondrous beauty defies description, surpasses even the sun, which will be increased sevenfold during the Millennium (Isa. 30:26). This city will have no need for the sun and moon, but the sun and moon will continue to shine for the sake of other parts of the Earth. The dazzling Light from the Glory of God shining out from this transparent city of gold will be beyond our present descriptive ability!

ACTIVITIES OF THE NATURAL PEOPLE

The gates of the New Jerusalem never will be closed in the eternal day of that city (Rev. 21:24-27). Natural men will live in various nations throughout the Earth, subject to the Eternal Kingdom ruled by God and the Saints forever. They will carry on natural activities, such as planting, harvesting, building, multiplying, and developing (Isa. 65:18-25). In their activities men will pass by the New Jerusalem and will visit the city. Leaders from various places in the Earth will come and give glory and honor to God in the Holy City, using the fruit of the Earth as an expression of love. The Holy City will be open, and whosoever will may come and visit with God personally!

RIVER OF LIFE

Water will be supplied abundantly in the city. Revelation 22 states that there will be a pure river of life proceeding out of the Throne of God:

"He showed me A PURE RIVER OF WATER OF LIFE, CLEAR AS CRYSTAL, PROCEEDING OUT OF THE THRONE OF GOD AND OF THE LAMB. . . . And the Spirit and the Bride say, Come. And let him that hears say, Come. And let him who is athirst come. And whosoever will, let him take the WATER OF LIFE freely" (Rev. 22:1, 17).

If the city is shaped like a mountain peak, or like a pyramid, which seems likely, the Thrones of God will be at the top, and the river will have a gradual flow for 1,500 miles from the top to the base of the city. This Scripture does not imply that these waters will be the means of Eternal Life, but water will be involved in the life-giving process. These waters are referred to as living fountains of water:

"The Lamb which is in the midst of the Throne shall feed them, and shall lead them unto LIVING FOUNTAINS OF WATERS: and God shall wipe away all tears from their eyes" (Rev. 7:17).

TREES OF LIFE

Revelation 22:2 states that in the middle of each of the twelve streets and on either side of the river there are trees of life. It appears that these streets are twelve great highways leading from the Throne to the twelve gates and that there will be a river of living water flowing down the middle of each street with the trees of life on either side. This quite naturally will mean that there will be twelve rivers as well as twelve streets and not just one street, one river, and one tree. It does refer to the nations eating of the tree, but the same language used regarding the street (singular) is used also with reference to the *"river."*

If there are twelve streets, then it is likely that there are twelve rivers, for just one river would not correspond with the rest of the Scripture. The word for *"river"* is translated in the plural in Revelation 8:10; 16:4; and the plural word for *"fountain"* is used in Revelation 7:17; 16:4.

HEALTII-GIVING FRUIT AND LEAVES

Each month these trees of life will bear a different kind of fruit. The leaves of the trees will serve to preserve the natural life of coming generations. This has nothing to do with the healing of sickness, pain, or like things of that nature, for the curse will have been lifted forever! The trees and rivers will be a distinct Divine provision for the pleasures of life for all peoples.

The residents of the New Jerusalem will enjoy the fruit of these trees, as was promised to the overcomer (Rev. 2:7; 22:14). The fruit will be also a source of enjoyment for the nations.

The leaves will be a provision from God for preservation of natural life and eternal health. Man will eat also of the *"hidden Manna"* (Rev. 2:17), the Passover Lamb, and drink of the fruit of the vine in the Father's Kingdom (Lk. 22:14-18). We shall sit down with the Lord and enjoy communion and fellowship with Him throughout all of the ages to come!

FULFILLMENT OF THE PLAN OF GOD

Thus, the Plan of God will be complete, for the Bible states, *"IT IS DONE"* (Rev. 21:6)! The longsuffering of God throughout the seven Dispensations of man's failure prove to us His Love for all mankind. We should not think that the future life eventually will become monotonous and wearisome, for this will be only the beginning of another Chapter in the Revelation of God to man. God will continue to work in and through man for His good pleasure. How thankful we will be that we have a part in the Eternal Plan of God!

"But God, WHO IS RICH IN MERCY, for His great Love wherewith He loved us, Even when we were dead in sins, has quickened us together with Christ, (BY GRACE YOU ARE SAVED;) And has raised us up together, and made us sit together in Heavenly Places in Christ Jesus: That in THE AGES TO COME HE MIGHT SHOW THE EXCEEDING RICHES OF HIS GRACE in His kindness toward us through Jesus Christ" (Eph. 2:4-7).

CONCLUSION

Dispensational Questions And Bible Answers

CONCLUSION

DISPENSATIONAL QUESTIONS AND BIBLE ANSWERS

1. *HOW OLD IS THE EARTH?*

The history of mankind extends back over 6,000 years. However, the Earth was created *"in the beginning"* (Gen. 1:1), which was some where in the dateless past. The Bible does not reveal the actual age of the Earth, although it is probably millions of years old, according to modern science.

2. *IS THERE LIFE ON OTHER PLANETS?*

Possibly so, for the Scriptures declare, *"REJOICE, YOU HEAVENS, AND YOU THAT DWELL IN THEM"* (Rev. 12:12). The Apostle Paul wrote, *"For by Him were all things created, that are IN HEAVEN, and that are in Earth, visible and invisible, whether they be THRONES, OR DOMINIONS, OR PRINCIPALITIES, OR POWERS: all things were created by Him, and for Him"* (Col. 1:16).

3. *WHY DID GOD NOT DESTROY LUCIFER WHEN HE FELL, RATHER THAN ALLOWING HIM TO BRING CORRUPTION AGAIN INTO THE WORLD?*

That Christ *"might destroy the works of the Devil"* (I Jn. 3:8). God allowed Satan to continue that He might show His Grace toward us in Salvation, healing, and Deliverance. When this purpose is completed, Satan will be *"cast into the Lake of Fire"* (Rev. 20:10).

4. *DID ADAM GO TO HELL BECAUSE OF HIS SIN?*

It is recorded that God gave Adam 120 additional years in which to repent for his sin (Gen. 6:3). Whether or not he did ask forgiveness is not revealed.

5. *WHAT HAPPENED TO THE DINOSAURS?*

Scientists tell us that the dinosaurs existed millions of years ago, which reveals that they were a part of the pre-Adamic world, over which Lucifer ruled as *"the anointed cherub"* (Ezek. 28:13-17). The dinosaurs perished in the flood of God's Judgment over the original perfect Earth, due to the fall of Lucifer and his subjects (Isa. 14:12-15; Jer. 4:23-26; Gen. 1:1-2; II Pet. 3:4-7).

6. *WHERE DID CAIN GET HIS WIFE?*

While the record in Scripture speaks only of Cain, Abel, and Seth by name, as being children of Adam and Eve, it is evident that Eve had other children also. Genesis 5:4 states, *"And the days of Adam after he had begotten Seth were eight hundred years: and he begat sons AND DAUGHTERS."* So Cain must have married a sister or niece, for all humanity descended from Adam and Eve.

7. *HOW IS THE SINFUL NATURE OF ADAM INHERITED?*

The Bible declares that as a result of Adam's disobedience *"sin entered into the world, and death by sin"* (Rom. 5:12). It says that *"by the offence of one judgment came upon all men to condemnation"* (Rom. 5:18). We have an inherited sinful nature because *"death passed upon all men, for that all have sinned"* (Rom. 5:12).

8. *WHAT HAPPENS TO A PERSON WHEN HE DIES?*

If a person is Born-Again, his spirit and soul go immediately to Heaven to be *"with the Lord"* (II Cor. 5:8). When Stephen was being stoned to death, he saw *"Jesus standing on the Right Hand of God"* ready to receive him into Heaven (Acts 7:55-56). The dead in Christ will remain in Heaven until the Rapture of the Church when the soul and spirit will be reunited with an incorruptible body at the First Resurrection (I Cor. 15:35-57; I Thess. 4:13-18; Rev. 20:6). After this the Glorified Saints of God will reign with Christ forever.

If a person is a sinner, his spirit and soul go immediately to Hell (Lk. 16:22-23), to remain in torment until the end of the Millennium (Rev. 20:5). After the thousand years, the soul and spirit will be reunited with an immortal body, to stand before the Great White Throne Judgment. After this wicked dead will be cast into the Lake of Fire (Rev. 20:11-15).

9. *HOW DID THERE BEGIN TO BE DIFFERENT RACES OF MEN?*

We do know that after the Flood, all men constituted of a single race, being the descendants of Noah's three sons (Gen. 9:18-19), and were located in one particular area of the Earth, which was one great land mass (Gen. 11:1). After the fall of the Tower of Babel the various languages came into being, and it stated that *"from thence did the LORD scatter them abroad upon the face of all the Earth"* (Gen. 11:1-9). Fourteen years prior to this a man named Peleg was born (Gen. 11:16), whose name meant *"earthquake."* During his lifetime it is recorded that the Earth was divided (Hebrew, *palag, "to split"* or *"divide"*) into continents. Each of the sons of Noah brought forth several nationalities (Gen. 10:1-32), who spread over the Earth, and then were divided into the various continents and islands.

10. *DOES GOD APPROVE OF CAPITAL PUNISHMENT?*

God *commanded* capital punishment for certain crimes *before* the Law (Gen. 9:5-6), *during* the Law (Ex. 21:12-14; Num. 35:30), and *after* the Law (Rom. 13:1-6). We have no reason to believe that God has changed His Plan concerning capital punishment, for it even will be an institution of the future Millennial Kingdom of Christ (Isa. 11:1-9; 65:20).

11. *WILL THE CHURCH GO THROUGH THE GREAT TRIBULATION?*

The Tribulation is described as *"the time of Jacob's trouble"* (Jer. 30:7), not the Church's. God told Daniel that the Tribulation would come upon His People, the Jews (Dan. 12:1). The Church never is mentioned in Scripture as passing through any part of the Tribulation. On the contrary, Jesus said that the Church would *"escape all these things that shall come to pass"* (Lk. 21:36). The Apostle Paul indicated that the Church would be taken out of the world *BEFORE "that Wicked be revealed"* (II Thess. 2:7-8), for *"God has not appointed us to wrath, but to obtain Salvation by our Lord Jesus Christ"* (I Thess. 5:9). The Church, in many parts of the world, *already* is experiencing great persecution and tribulation! The Church in America has been greatly blessed! But to say that the Church must pass through the Tribulation to be purified is unscriptural. The Church already has been made pure by the Blood of Christ!

12. *WHY DID OLD TESTAMENT PERSONS LIVE SO LONG?*

No doubt it was due to the fact that the Earth was not polluted as it is in our day. Also, the diet God prescribed at the beginning was much healthier than most menus (Gen. 1:29; 9:3-4). In the Millennium men once again will live to be hundreds of years old (Isa. 65:20) and in the New Earth will live *forever* (Rev. 21:4).

13. *CAN SATAN READ YOUR MIND?*

Satan is not omniscient; thus, he is limited in his knowledge as all of the rest of God's creation. God alone is all-knowing (I Jn. 3:20).

14. *WILL WE KNOW EACH OTHER IN HEAVEN?*

Yes, for this is clear from I Corinthians 13:12, "(We shall) *know even as also* (we are) *known!*"

15. *WILL WE BE ABLE TO SEE GOD THE FATHER, GOD THE SON, AND GOD THE HOLY SPIRIT IN HEAVEN?*

Yes, *"Blessed are the pure in heart: for THEY SHALL SEE GOD"* (Mat. 5:8). *"The Throne of God AND of the Lamb shall be in it; and His servants shall serve Him: AND THEY SHALL SEE HIS FACE"* (Rev. 22:3-4).

16. *DOES I PETER 3:21 NOT TEACH THAT WATER BAPTISM SAVES US?*

Peter there explained that baptism is *"NOT the putting away of the filth of the flesh, but the ANSWER of a good conscience toward God."* If a person looks to water to save him, he will be lost! If he looks to Christ to save him, and in baptism acknowledges Christ as his Saviour, his Salvation will be through Christ and not through the virtue of water.

17. *CAN A CHRISTIAN BE DEMON POSSESSED?*

Absolutely not! *"He who is begotten of God keeps himself, AND THAT WICKED ONE TOUCHES HIM NOT"* (I Jn. 5:18). *"GREATER IS HE WHO IS IN YOU, THAN HE WHO IS IN THE WORLD"* (I Jn. 4:4).

18. *IS GAMBLING A SIN?*

The Bible says, *"You shall do no unrighteousness in judgment, in meteyard, in weight, or in measure. Just balances, just weights, a just ephah, and a just hin"* (Lev. 19:35-36). We are to *earn* our wages (Eph. 4:28; II Thess. 3:10) through hard work! Gambling cheats others, and the Scriptures command us not to *"defraud"* other people (I Cor. 6:7-8; I Thess. 4:6).

19. *IS HELL REALLY A PLACE OF ETERNAL FIRE AND TORMENT?*

Jesus made it plain that the rich man in Hell was being *"tormented in this flame"* (Lk. 16:24). We have no reason to spiritualize the language, for there are scores of Scriptures stating that Hell is a place burning with *"fire and brimstone"* (Lk. 16:19-31; Mk. 9:43-48; Rev. 14:9-11; 20:10-15; *et al*).

20. *WHAT IS THE MARK OF THE BEAST?*

No one will know until the mark is given (Rev. 13:16-18) during the second half of the Tribulation. We do know that the *number* of the Beast will be 666 (Rev. 13:18).

21. *WHAT WAS PAUL'S THORN IN THE FLESH?*

The Scripture passage where this is mentioned tells us plainly that the thorn was *"the messenger of Satan"* (II Cor. 12:7). The word *"messenger"* in the Greek is *aggelos* or *"Angel,"* implying that a fallen Angel followed Paul causing afflictions such as shipwrecks, imprisonment, beatings, etc.

22. *MUST A PERSON SPEAK IN OTHER TONGUES IN ORDER TO BE SAVED?*

Absolutely not! Salvation is received by Repentance toward God and Faith in Jesus Christ (Rom. 10:9-10). The Baptism with the Holy Spirit, with the initial, physical evidence of speaking with other tongues, is an experience *subsequent* to the new birth (Acts 1:5; 2:38-39; 19:1-6).

SELF-HELP STUDY NOTES